SEEKING EAST

SEEKING EAST

....

AN EXPAT FAMILY'S
YEAR IN HONG KONG

SAM OLSEN

Inkstone
Books

www.samolsenasia.com

Author's Note: Hong Kong is a small place. In the event that some people might not want their foibles and actions revealed through my clumsy hand, a few names have been altered and one or two events merged. But the spirit remains true.

Ordering Information:
Quantity sales. Special discounts are available on quantity purchases by corporations, associations, and others. For details, contact the "Special Sales Department" at the address above.

Distributed by Inkstone Books
http://inkstone.chameleonpress.com

Seeking East/ Samuel Hatlem Olsen. -- 1st ed.
ISBN 978-988-13974-1-6

To Aggie, Lawrence and Dominic,
my fellow Eastern adventurers

All things are difficult before they are easy.

ONE

....

Given that it was an innocuous Tuesday evening in rush-hour Oxford Circus I hadn't expected to be punched in the face, so my reactions were pretty slow. Luckily he was a rubbish shot, and all he managed was a glancing blow to my eye that left us both unbalanced, halfway down the tube station escalator. Rather than reply tit-for-tat, I leaned forward, put him in a headlock, and sat on his sallow, white-jacketed body as he screamed muffled profanities at me and clawed at my suit trousers.

The whole thing started when the unpleasant youth I now sat on barged down the packed line of commuters pushing everyone out of his way, including the heavily pregnant woman in front of me who was almost jettisoned over the handrail. Instinctively, I made a two-handed lunge, one to right the woman and one to grab her assailant's jacket. I mumbled some sort of warning as I made contact, with the result that he turned around and walloped me in the face.

Soon we reached the end of the escalator. This forced me to stand up and release my temporary prisoner, who sprang to his feet and immediately raised his fists to continue what he'd started. Unfortunately he was no longer alone. Five hooded and threatening lads had joined their friend and were standing in a semicircle around me, with the look of a hyena pack in a zebra nursery. It was not looking overly comfortable.

A second later they were gone, alerted by the shouting of the police officers running down the escalators behind me. I had never been so pleased to see half a dozen uniformed men. They sprinted past in pursuit of the thugs, leaving me and the pregnant woman standing by the wall, breathing a bit faster than we had been only a few minutes before. I headed back upstairs and took the bus instead.

The next morning I was standing on a train platform, waiting to start my two-hour daily commute, with a slightly reddened eye and exceedingly wet legs, as the rain poured around the periphery of my umbrella. The train was delayed, so when it finally came the carriage was even more crowded than normal, giving me the pleasure of multiple armpits in my face. I was thoroughly bad-tempered by the time I reached my office, a mood not helped by the news that we had lost a major client. It was not a good twenty-four hours, and that night I returned home to my wife Aggie a thoroughly annoyed man.

Our lives had become hollow in a way that we'd always sworn we would never let happen; reduced to a tedious commute and the constant burden of paying the bills, occasionally enlivened by a touch of street crime. As we had just had our first child, we were also trying to find a way of affording flexible childcare so we would both be able to continue our careers. The sums were ridiculous, and we would only just be covering our costs to have our son looked after, which of course meant no ability at all to save for the future.

To make matters worse, our friends were leaving London in a steady flood. Only the week before, we had been to the latest leaving party, saying goodbye to yet another couple who had decided that a quiet life in the country was preferable to the freneticism of a capital city. Gone were the post-work pints in the pub; people were either catching the train out of the city or, if they were still living in London, were heading home early to put junior to bed. It was a far cry from only a few years before, when we ranged across the bars of Camden and Kentish Town, unweighted by any thought of familial responsibility and only a few minutes stagger from home. Age and parenthood had taken their socialising toll and so, together with our work and money lives, our quality of life had significant room for improvement.

Imagine therefore my immense relief when one night I returned home, shattered but ready for a long night looking after the baby, to be told that we had been given a golden ticket to a new world.

TWO

....

My first view of Hong Kong was of a middle-aged Chinese woman hanging up her washing. Given that she was at eye level, two hundred feet away, and rushing past at several hundred miles an hour, this was a somewhat unusual introduction to the place. Yet in 1996, this was the approach the old city centre airport demanded, the plane threading its way through skyscrapers and hoping that the runway didn't run out before the plane stopped. The fact that only two hundred or so people had died landing or taking off was not a major comfort, but it was an experience to remember, if not necessarily to savour.

With a landing like that there was no choice but to go and find a drink. Graham, a blonde-haired friend from university and my travelling companion on this first visit to Hong Kong, led the way to what he assured me was a good place to start. I had vaguely heard of Wanchai, but nothing prepared me for the sights and sounds I experienced that night. Warm-faced Asian girls—tight in both miniskirt and boobtube—lined the street, beckoning passers-by into their madams' speakeasies. Their marks followed them like drunken moths to a naked flame. Soldiers from the British Garrison, identifiable by their uniform of cropped hair, white untucked t-shirts, and blue, ironed jeans, stumbled along the pavement, ping-ponging off parked cars and lamp-posts as wary locals moved aside. Traffic fumes wallowed in the air, giving the scene a lead-lined whiff and searing the lungs of the smokers who filled the road-side bars. It was early evening but Saturday night was peaking already.

Not quite ready for the full show, Graham and I moved around the corner to a quieter street. We swung open the door of a pub, slipped into the darkness, and took our first real breath of a Wanchai watering hole. It was the smell of cigarettes and beer, the sizzle of fried meat, and the tang of spilt whiskey soaking into the broad wooden bar. In other words, it was the aroma of a good night out. We certainly enjoyed ourselves, mixing with everyone from bearded old China hands to red-cheeked young squaddies, and Chinese women far too old and pretty for us. At around 8am I lost Graham to a Kiwi girl so cut my losses and headed home, sporting an extraordinarily broad grin at the thought of several more weeks of this.

The rest of our time in Hong Kong was just as rewarding, our days spent hiking or sightseeing or sleeping, our nights hopping between a variety of hot spots. It was everything I had hoped for—and far, far more—ever since my infatuation with Hong Kong had started as a boy. This was when my father went there for a rare business trip. I well remember his homecoming, pitching up at the front door with his trademark burgundy suitcase and carrying in his hands presents for me and my sister. We ripped open the packaging with untold excitement to find we had each received what appeared to be some kind of vegetative pith helmet.

"It's a bamboo hat," Dad explained, looking rather pleased with himself. "You wear it when you're working in the sun." It was all very confusing for a young boy from the cloudy English countryside, and even more so when the rattan furniture arrived. For some reason he had decided that a full set of Hong Kong-style bamboo tables and chairs would be the best thing for our home. While this would have been perfect if had we suddenly been descended upon by a couple of dozen Chinese folk seriously picky about what they sat on, it was a furniture choice that was a bit of a surprise for rural Leicestershire. Yet despite the abnormality of the souvenirs they were enough to pique my curiosity, especially when put alongside the photos he brought back, of dancing dragons, flapping chickens at market, and sleek wooden red-sailed junks. Hong Kong seemed at once both highly exotic and demonstrably accessible, and from that moment I was smitten.

My first trip was a decade after my father's, and timed to see the then British-ruled colony in the last few months before it was reunited with the Chinese Motherland. Apart from having an exceptionally fun time, I also learnt a great deal about the place.

The first lesson was geography. Being subtropical and monsoonal, the weather was a good deal sprightlier than in the UK. This was evidenced by the typhoons that regularly came barrelling in, sometimes causing horrendous damage, especially in days past. It was also a lot warmer, which to someone as cold-blooded as me was a wonderful perk.

Size-wise, the territory was around two-thirds the size of Greater London but with a similar population, and was spread across three main areas: Hong Kong Island, Kowloon, and the New Territories. All in all there were around two hundred and sixty islands, most of which were uninhabited. Hong Kong Island, a mountainous fist of land about the size of Manhattan, was the first part of the territory to be won by the British and was the centre of official and commercial life. It was also where most expats—gweilos (for men) and gweipors (for women)—spent their days. Victoria Harbour, which was forever shrinking thanks to perennial reclamation, separated the island from the peninsular of Kowloon. Meaning 'nine dragons' on account of the nine hills that delineated it from the land further north, Kowloon was a cheaper and therefore more highly populated place to live, with a staggering population density of three hundred and forty thousand people per square mile. In contrast, the New Territories, wedged between Kowloon and the border with China-proper, were less populated and even had the occasional farm. With nearly ten thousand people per square mile, it was almost as crowded as Gibraltar.

The second lesson I learnt was that, despite a hundred and fifty years of British rule, it was much more Chinese than English. I had, for some naïve and hard to fathom reason, always imagined it to be a piece of Home Counties stuck out East, perhaps passing a vague resemblance to Dorking or Sevenoaks surrounded by rice paddies. But while the British influence was still very strong, the fact that over ninety percent of its population were Chinese meant that it was by necessity much more Canton than Camden. What was also noticeable was that, while nearly everyone spoke English, there was a distinct range of linguistic ability in the language. Taxi drivers would know a couple of phrases, whereas if you went to a bar and spoke to the Chinese person next to you they would probably be absolutely fluent in Shakespeare's tongue. It was certainly not a straightforward place to understand.

Interestingly, the language challenge was made even harder as the local dialect of Cantonese, whilst using the same standard Chinese script, sounded as different to Mandarin as French did to German. This led to the peculiar thought that whilst a Cantonese speaker and a Mandarin speaker could read and understand the same newspaper, they couldn't actually talk to each other. Graham and I had made a mistake by preparing for our trip with Mandarin lessons, not that we lasted long. After a half-dozen sessions our teacher politely asked us to leave the class rather than hold back the more gifted students; at the time we were a bit embarrassed by our ineptitude, but given the uselessness of the language in Hong Kong we were pretty grateful to her in the end.

The third, and possibly the most memorable, lesson was that Hong Kong was seriously fun. Its melange of East and West meant that there was an endless buffet of Chinese traditions and customs, theme parks, local cuisine, and verdant countryside to beguile the visitor. The nightlife was especially entertaining, as Wanchai had shown. But this wasn't the only place to be at night. There were several other nightlife zones, and none more famous than Lan Kwai Fong. It was one man, a Canadian-German named Alan Zeman, who turned LKF from a place known for hawkers and rubbish bags into Hong Kong's premier night-zone, and all because he wasn't satisfied with his options when dining out. In 1984 he founded a restaurant called California, which did quite well and so inspired him to buy up the surrounding dilapidated buildings. The result was millions of dollars of profit for him and plenty of good nights out for the rest of us.

Zeman taught me another lesson, that there was a great deal of money to be made here. This was brought home to me when I arranged to meet a distant cousin in one of LKF's more colourful bars, Yeltsin, a kitsch homage to the Soviet Union with a neat and obvious line in vodka. He had come out just after university as a penniless graduate, and now after only a decade was thoroughly rich and decadently happy. Graham and I accepted his hospitality without a moment's guilt and enjoyed every moment of it.

The final lesson I learnt from my trip was that there was much more to Hong Kong than wealth. That it was rich was clear: as the renowned restaurant critic A. A. Gill once noted put it, Hong Kong was "a temple to Mammon, booming and fit to burst", and "as fat and self-satisfied as any city could be". Yet it was a schizophrenic place, both gritty port and refined cultural hub. A backdrop for paintings, a muse for books, and a setting for movies; where thousands of modern, American-style skyscrapers rubbed alongside classic colonial architecture and concrete Chinese-style houses. It was the home of both the über-wealthy and the incredibly underprivileged, such as the ancient, craggy women pushing rubbish carts up hills past twenty-five-year-old men already making their second fortune. There was a depth that would take many lifetimes to fully explore.

Indeed, my trip with Graham was a fantastic introduction to Hong Kong, but I felt that I had only scratched the surface. I would spend the next decade and a half wanting to make the place home, and so when my wife's company offered to move us there we took the opportunity very seriously indeed.

The reasons for moving there were more than just happy memories and a long-standing desire though; our current married and parenting selves had many reasons to consider relocating. Friends of ours that had lived in Hong Kong reported it as a veritable paradise for working with a young family.

For a start, childcare was cheap, and when our son was older the educational system was meant to be top-notch too, especially as it would mean him learning the language of the hour, Chinese. For the family as a whole there was plenty to do, with beaches and jungle and mountains, and shops and museums and sport, not to mention the innumerable bars and restaurants all within easy reach of home, given the small size of the territory.

In terms of work, it was reported that there was an abundance of well-paid jobs, unlike the busted flush that was the British economy at that time. So although I would be arriving there without gainful employment, I'd be sure to find work soon enough.

All in all, as a fine place to raise a child, with ready access to adventure and entertainment, and with more money to save and spend, Hong Kong seemed to be an excellent place to move to.

The only flies in the ointment were our parents. They were not going to be overly smitten with our plans as we would be taking their new pride and conversation piece—our son—to the other side of the world. Sure enough, there were a few tears at the thought of us leaving the UK with their grandson, but there were also the more general worries too. What would happen if I couldn't find a job? What if we became ill? What if we couldn't make a social life for ourselves? There were, it seemed, many reasons why emigrating could be a bad idea, and we were warned not to take these risks lightly.

So, in the end, we came up with a compromise. We would give it a year, and if we weren't truly happier there, then we would come back to the UK and reclaim our old lives. With our parents satisfied, and the clock ticking, we closed one chapter of our lives and prepared to open a very different Eastern one."

THREE

....

As our parents warned us, not all expat moves to Hong Kong
ended well. Rob Kissel, a wealthy American banker, took this
to the extreme when he ended up being poisoned and murdered in a joint family hit a few years after arriving in Hong Kong.

To the outside world everything looked rosy with the Kissels; a fun,
social couple with three cute kids. Unfortunately, his wife Nancy was a
maniac. Although she was described as high-maintenance before her
move to Hong Kong, it was whilst stuck out in the wealthy enclave of
Parkview that insanity started to take hold. She demonstrated her slip
from reality by having an affair with a TV installer called Michael Del
Priore whilst on a break to their home in America. It would be fair to say
that she threw herself wholeheartedly into infidelity, calling her lover
dozens of times a day, often on call-collect. This was understandable
from a secretive point of view, but it did land Del Priore with a
US$20,000 bill, a sum he could ill afford as he was living in a trailer park.

Nancy's attempts to keep the affair a secret failed when Rob came
across her correspondence with Del Priore on the computer, and then
hired a private detective to follow her. Soon he had proof and decided to
sue for divorce, which is where he made a mistake that would cost him
his life; Rob accidentally faxed a list of divorce lawyers to his home rather than to his office, giving Nancy a pretty obvious clue as to his intentions.

She knew the game was up and, with an $18 million inheritance in the balance, decided to strike first. Her twisted modus operandi was to first incapacitate her husband, which she did by lacing his milkshake with enough sedatives to knock out an ox. Knowing that he would be highly suspicious of a random act of kindness from his philandering wife, she persuaded her six-year-old daughter to give him the milkshake. Later, while he was passed out cold, she bludgeoned him to death with a lead statuette. Being a spoilt expat wife, she rolled up his body in a rug and then made the building's handyman carry the package to the basement for storage. Not surprisingly, she was sentenced to life imprisonment.

Needless to say, I hadn't discussed the case in too much detail with my wife, given that I was going to be the one at home with the family, at least in the short term. It did however make me sure never to get too bored and crazy—a possibility that soon appeared slim as I realised that Hong Kong was still the chaotic and vibrant maelstrom that I remembered.

We arrived on a Wednesday morning. A white-shirted driver was there to meet us at arrivals, helping to cram our oversized luggage into his silver Asian Utility Vehicle, before setting off into the traffic with a flurry of Cantonese that we could only smile at. Although the new airport had originally been built some distance out of town we were surrounded by residential towers within a few minutes of our drive. As we drove over the suspension bridge towards Central, the main hub of Hong Kong and our new temporary home, the concrete and steel of forty thousand buildings jutting into the sky filled the horizon. This was going to be slightly different from North London.

My wife's work had been kind enough to arrange for us to stay for a month in a serviced apartment a few minutes' walk from her new office. We were met by the building's concierge, a short Chinese man with a long, narrow face, black hair with a side parting, and a white short-sleeved shirt that covered an obvious pigeon chest.

"My name is Wing. Nice to meet you," he said, holding out his hand to give us a hand lugging the bags to the lift. "You have many luggage," he puffed ruefully.

Called Central 88—partly because eight is a lucky number in Chinese, partly because it was actually located at 88 Des Voeux Road—the two-bedroom flat was nice, small, but very, very urban. It had only one window, and that faced a brick wall, so it was not particularly set up for people from the countryside or the suburbs. But the furniture was clean, there were no obvious stains, and there was a TV the size of a small planet. It would do.

The best thing about the flat was that it was next to a bun shop. Not the patisseries of Paris or Vienna you understand, but a typical Hong Kong place, with barbeque pork buns, pineapple buns, custard buns, tuna buns; every sweet or savoury combination you could imagine. For $20—about £1.80—you could buy one of these treats, hoping that the taste wouldn't be overshadowed by severe food poisoning later.

Within an hour of moving in we had eaten what felt like dozens of buns, gorging in front of the TV while flicking through local soap operas and the global news stations. We then emptied our suitcases, cursing loudly as we remembered what we had forgotten, and made ourselves feel at home.

Feeling a bit more organised, and with our travel-hunger sated, it was time to go out exploring. We had been told by Wing that there was a typhoon warning in place—how exotic—so we grasped our umbrellas in the hope that they would be sufficient to ward off winds and rain strong enough to sink a fleet. For the meantime we were happy to take a chance and look around.

Our neighbourhood streets felt like stream beds carved into huge canyons of steel and glass, and every few yards we'd be subjected to a new olfactory sensation, like the powerful cooking oil aroma that exuded from every restaurant and which was nothing like we had back in England. Everywhere we looked there were people. We had chosen to explore at lunchtime, so the pavements were busier than a mosh pit, pedestrians pushing past the café and restaurant queues that piled up around the blocks. The pushchair of our son, Larry, was not proving to be a convenient accessory to the walk.

Yet funnily enough it didn't feel as foreign as it might have. Straight out in front of Central 88 was the first reminder that Hong Kong was not such a strange country for Britons. A large red double-decker bus chugged by, an image straight out of Holborn although full of friendly Chinese faces, rather than the haunted, sickly beings that tend to inhabit London's bus network. A bell rang and we saw a tram heading in the opposite direction, its sides plastered with advertising for what appeared to be constipation relief or something equally medical—the grimace of the poster woman was hard to fathom. All we needed now was a Hackney cab and we could have been in 1950s Piccadilly Circus, with the fumes to match.

Despite the chronic air pollution, mixed with high humidity and a stupefying heat—it felt like we were in an oven that had just been sprayed with diesel—we were supremely content in our first few hours there.

However, when we awoke on our second day things felt a little different. Perhaps it was the lingering jet lag that kept all three of us up throughout the night, but the novelty started to wear off quickly.

We started to feel a little claustrophobic. It is impossible from a Western sense to emphasise how crowded Central is. Its pavements are crammed full of people from before dawn to after dusk. The situation is made worse by the chronic dawdling that seems to befuddle everyone; perhaps stopping to stare at a poster, or look at their phones, or just have a chat. Then there are the local workers who get in everyone's way, pushing along large industrial trolleys at less than a mile an hour. Add to all this traffic lights that take forever—with hardly anyone crossing the road unless there is a green man—and walking around takes a long time.

To be precise, three minutes to walk two hundred yards, as I one day measured.

Another worry was the realisation that time was ticking. Central 88 was our home for only a short time, so we had to start looking for a flat immediately. Then there was all the admin to do, like getting our ID cards sorted, and registering our driving licences—in fact, all the jobs that no one really likes doing at all, never mind all at once and in a foreign country. With my wife only having a couple of days to find her feet before work started, the burden was going to fall on me.

FOUR

....

Ut the admin could wait. Faced with a list and a half of things
to do, and feeling slightly overwhelmed by the crowds, we decided to put everything on hold and get out of Central for the
day. We rose early to catch the fast and comfortable ferry to Lantau, the
large isle to the West of Hong Kong Island and the home of the new
airport, a giant Buddha, and eighteen thousand people living in a remake
of Jim Carrey's 1998 film The Truman Show. Discovery Bay, or DB, or
even Disco Bay as it was known, was a place where nothing went wrong.
As cars were banned, residents—mostly gweilos or Western-born Chinese—used golf buggies to drive past the perfect beach and the perfect
house developments, all called things like 'Seabee Lane' or 'Bijou Hamlet', on their way to one of the four private clubs, or to the identikit restaurants that perched on the waterfront. It felt like Disneyland, which by
chance happened to be just a couple of miles away.

DB was designed for someone who wanted to pretend that they lived
in suburban America, surrounded only by English-speaking golf fanatics,
and living a life as exciting as a beige Renault Clio. Given that we had
moved away from Britain partly to have an adventure, living in DB really
didn't appeal. We finished our perfect cappuccinos and fled on the next
ferry out of there.

The plan had been to visit a Trappist monastery just around the corner from DB—an idea born out of a look at the guidebook rather than

16

any personal connection to monks—but we were in such a rush to get out of the Truman Show that we screwed up our itinerary. Our ferry instead took us to tiny Peng Chau, a small island between Lantau and Hong Kong, which felt far less artificial, starting with the ferry. Rather than a sleek, fibreglass vessel, this was a battered old wooden affair, with no window glass or air conditioning. It was crewed by an old, hunch-backed woman in a bamboo hat and dark, dusty clothes who sat and stared at us the whole journey long. Once we were on Peng Chau we noticed straightaway that there were no modern buildings, apart from a concrete toilet block, and a distinct lack of non-Chinese faces. It was the antithesis of Discovery Bay, but only a few minutes away by sea.

A downside to this 'authenticity' was the lack of a cold drink anywhere. We searched high and low for a café to sit down in, but all the seats were taken—indeed there were deep queues—so soon our tempers began to fray. At last we did find a water-seller, but were forced to sit in the baking sun and slowly frazzle amidst the throng. We soon realised what the crush was about, as we saw what appeared to be boy scouts preparing some costumes and enormous drums. A passer-by, a bespectacled Chinese woman with a tight black perm and a pink t-shirt, stopped to say hello to our son as we admired the preparations.

"It's about Tin Hau," she said, in a slight American accent, "the Goddess of the Sea. Each year she moves out of her temple, and travels around the island blessing all the fishermen. Then her figure goes back into her temple."

I thanked her for her insight, and asked if she was a local to know so much.

"Oh no, I live in San Francisco. I just read about this in a magazine."

This admission made us question whether her description was exactly what we were watching, but it was highly interesting all the same. All the shops had dishes of fruit and burning candles in the doorways, although to be honest some were shops, some were people's houses—we couldn't tell the difference. Then at 1pm the parade began, and what a racket it was. There was a constant banging of drums and cymbals, with hundreds of flags and papier-mâché silvery fish on the ends of poles. The dragons were a little scary when they came up close, with even the locals backing away, although I was glad to note that Larry was unperturbed when one particularly lively dragon approached him.

Soon the parade had passed and, although we followed it for a while, the crowds were too thick for us to really see anything so we decided to head home. It was a quiet ferry ride back to Central, with Larry asleep and my wife smiling from ear to ear.

"That was pretty good fun, wasn't it?"

Sadly, the days that followed brought us back to reality. Hong Kong may have been a deep reservoir of adventure, but we also needed to live. I required a job, and as I wouldn't be able to properly search for gainful employment until I was freed up from full-time parental responsibilities, we had to find some suitable childcare too.

It soon became clear that the advice we'd been given back in the UK was correct, in that the vast majority of middle class Hong Kongers had permanent babysitting on tap in the form of live-in helpers. Indeed, there were hundreds of thousands of domestic helpers in Hong Kong, as anyone that walked around Central on a Sunday would immediately notice. Every pavement, overpass, and even road was crammed with sheets of cardboard, upon which were perched countless numbers of helpers—ninety-nine percent of them women—from either the Philippines or Indonesia. Gathered in small groups, they mostly just chatted whilst eating from enormous platters of rice with chicken, fish, or plantains. Some of them would be brushing or cutting hair, others listening to music or arranging themselves into compact dance groups and entertaining themselves with steps to the left and right. This was how the helpers spent their days off.

Up until thirty years previously, helpers were a perk that very few could afford. Traditionally the role of maid-cum-cleaner-cum-babysitter was held by professional Cantonese women called 'may je' who were known for their long, braided hair and distinctive black and white outfits. But by the time of the 1980s most were coming up to retirement age, and the younger generations had made enough money from the booming economy to want to hire helpers, rather than be helpers themselves.

Hong Kongers instead started to import labour from abroad, starting with the Philippines. Until President Marcos and his shoe-loving wife, Imelda, got their corrupt hands on power, the Philippines had been one of the wealthiest countries in Asia, and had actually imported thousands of Chinese helpers over the years. Yet now it was in more straitened circumstances, and possessed a glut of unemployed women who were glad to relocate for work. They were followed in turn by Indonesians, Indians, Nepalese, Bangladeshis, Sri Lankans, and a whole host of nationalities that were keen to swap the grind of subsistence living for the perceived glamour of Hong Kong.

To Western eyes it would seem odd, even immoral, to leave your family and, more often than not, your children to move to a foreign country and look after a stranger's house. This is a point of view that doesn't take into account the significant advantage that working abroad has given these women. To put this advantage in context, a helper paid at the minimum wage in Hong Kong earns the same as a provincial mayor in the Philippines, with the extra advantage of nearly all expenses being paid. This means that a year of saving in Hong Kong would equate to around twenty years of saving in Manila, and with a significantly reduced likelihood of being a victim of crime to boot. No wonder so many Filipinas want to work overseas.

That isn't to say that helpers always had it easy, as an imaginatively nicknamed Cantonese couple called Mr and Mrs Evil showed. They were found guilty of inflicting a series of wounds on their Indonesian helper, using 'clothes hangers, shoes and a bicycle chain' over a two-year period. Ironically, the wife was a hospital care worker, but this didn't stop her taking the lead in the assaults, which included wounding her charge with a paper cutter and an iron. There were also stories of helpers being made to sleep on the sofa or even on the kitchen floor, and given a food allowance of just one egg a day, however, the vast majority had a friendly family to work with.

We were extraordinarily lucky in finding the most perfect helper possible within a few days of looking. We had used an agency to help us find a suitable candidate or two, which had been an experience in itself. Walking into the office, which resembled a Hollywood Private Eye's with its glass door, black antique phones, and square wooden desks, Larry was soon whisked away from me by a gang of cooing Filipinas while I filled in the paperwork. We interviewed around a dozen women, all extremely nice but many of them not quite fitting the bill, including the one that turned up in a skirt shorter than a standard belt and who touched my leg several times while avoiding the gaze of Aggie. I have no idea why she was vetoed.

Happily our interviews also produced Tessie, a married Filipina with two grown-up children and a quiet manner that juxtaposed well with our family noise. When all the forms and her visa were sorted, she was ready to move in with us. But first we had to find somewhere to live.

FIVE

....

Hong Kong's economy is built on property. Ever since an early British governor realised that a good way to raise revenue was through the one resource Hong Kong had—land— buildings have been a ready source of cash. This had the effect of making the housing sector incredibly competitive, as demand always outstripped supply. Even without the capitalistic advantage of keeping the supply short, there was always going to be intense pressure thanks to the sheer number of people living here. In 1910, the population of Hong Kong was four hundred and thirty-six thousand, but when we arrived it was officially just under eight million, although many estimated that if you included all the illegal immigrants, mainly from the People's Republic of China next door, then the figure was more like ten.

All these people need somewhere to live. Given that Hong Kong, with a similar population to London, has thirty percent less land, the only way to build was up. In actual fact, it has about sixty percent less land, because around half of Hong Kong's territory is national park and can't be built on. It's probably the only place in the world where property developers actually like do-gooder tree-huggers. We heard it said that there were nearly eight thousand high-rise buildings in Hong Kong, including more than fifty skyscrapers over six hundred and fifty feet high, and two hundred and seventy over five hundred feet—all a world record. It really was a land of giants. Yet this unique skyline was all comparatively recent.

21

Jardine House, a five hundred and eighty-five foot edifice at the heart of the Central waterfront owned by the prominent Anglo company Jardine Mathesons, was the tallest building in both Hong Kong and Asia when it was completed in 1972. Nowadays there were hundreds of buildings that dwarfed it across the East.

The complexity of building all these towers was nothing like trying to find a home in one. The scale was intimidating; Taikoo Shing, a development on the north of Hong Kong Island built on an old dock, housed three times more people than live in the Leicestershire town of Market Harborough where I grew up, and had twelve thousand six hundred and ninety-eight apartments to choose from.

It became quite clear that we were going to need some expert help to guide us through the nightmare of finding a flat. Into this role stepped Rita. In her mid-fifties, but like most Chinese women looking at least ten years younger, she had wavy, black, shoulder-length hair, a warm smile, and the ability to speak at three hundred words a minute and still be understood.

"Helloooo Larry and Larry parents," she would rattle as we climbed into her car, her driver waiting for the untold number of instructions that would change every other minute.

"I think we go to Belcher apartment now, then Pokfulam area later...yes, that would be good," and she would bark something at John (all her drivers were called John), who would check the mirror and swing the steering wheel around, but not necessarily in that order. Toots would sound as we mounted the kerb on our one hundred and eighty degree turn and headed back to where we'd been only minutes before.

Looking around properties in Hong Kong was a bit different to back home. For a start, there wasn't even the remotest sniff of landing a house, unless you wanted to live in the northern New Territories or had a lot of money to spend. A quick search on a local property website for 'detached house' revealed that the cheapest was available for £110,000 a year to rent. I mean, seriously? Two minutes of research confirmed that it's not actually possible to spend that much on a house in Hull.

That said, flats still weren't cheap. One thing that we thought may have worked in our favour was that the Chinese seem to be obsessed with 'new', so some of the older flats—where we really didn't mind living—provided a lot more value for money.

The fact that there were so many apartments in Hong Kong meant that people could be quite fussy about all the potential added extras; perks that would have been well out of reach for us back in Britain. Did we want a gym in our building? A swimming pool? A shuttle bus to take us to work in the morning and bring us back at night?

All these options addled our brains. Looking for flats in London had been more about where the nearest tube station was, and potentially if there was a park nearby. How would we cope with the choice we now faced?

We soon entered into a home-hunting routine. We would arrive at a block of flats and wait while Rita discussed something in Cantonese with the austere concierge that blocked our way. Once Rita had spoken to them for a minute or two, had signed an official form or three, and cracked a couple of dozen smiles, we would all be herded into the lift. A number of seconds would pass while Rita remembered which floor we were going to, and then with a flourish she would press the right button. Once there a huge bunch of keys would be produced, reminiscent of a mediaeval gaoler, and we would wait a few minutes more for her to find us a way to unlock the door. Then with shoes removed, in keeping with the home tradition of Hong Kong, we would enter.

For the first few flats we spent a fair bit of time inside, looking at the amount of storage available, checking to see if the kitchen actually had any appliances (ovens, for instance, were extremely rare as the Chinese didn't have a need for them in their home cooking), and absorbing the view. Each cupboard would be opened, every tap turned on, all rooms measured to check the beds would fit in. Larry would meanwhile be crawling around the invariably wooden floors, keeping Rita entertained and allowing us to ponder in peace.

After a dozen or so visits this went out the window. We were tired, thirsty, and getting a tad flustered by our inability to see something that both met our still undefined criteria and which we could afford. Rita kept on smiling throughout, obviously a bit more used to the whole experience.

One day, as our patience really was starting to wear thin, Rita came bounding into the hallway of Central 88 with a definitive smile on her face.

"You will like what I have found for you today. I am sure." And to be fair, we would have done if the landlord hadn't been dead.

The flat, lying in the western suburb of Pokfulam, was indeed all we could have asked for. Apart from looking like it had been decorated by a fan of That '70s Show it was spacious, with a large balcony and unobstructed views of the sea. The sitting room was thirty-two feet long, an absolutely unheard of figure for Hong Kong unless you had a few million (pounds, sadly) to spare.

And here lay the problem: it was too cheap. In other words, we could afford it. I asked Rita why as we drove back to Central, and she was unsure.

"Sometimes you get lucky." That sounded good to us. Then everything started to unravel.

The next day Larry and I were dispatched by my suspicious wife to have a final check of the place before submitting an offer. We were met at the door by a woman straight out of Chinese Jerry Springer; high heels, short black shirt, a tight t-shirt asking someone to 'Love Me', and with enough make-up to stock the Revlon warehouse for six years. In her arms was a small hound that looked like a mix between a Chihuahua and a badger, sporting a doggie baseball jacket. It was a bizarre combination.

I asked her if she was the landlady. She looked at me and grinned. Rita asked again, this time in Cantonese. A flurry of conversation and a few raised eyebrows later, and Rita turned to me.

"She does not own the flat."

"Well who does?"

"Someone who is no longer with us."

In other words, he was Delta Echo Alpha Delta. He was an ex-landlord.

Back home, having extricated ourselves from the presence of the walking mannequin, we did some Googling. Apparently the landlord, one of Hong Kong's richest men thanks to a fortune built on taxis, had actually died ten years before. His estate had been in limbo ever since, as his children, all sixteen of them, and his three mistresses fought over the legacy. It turned out that one of the mistresses had decided to go free-lance and start renting out some of her erstwhile lover's property, proba-bly to pay the legal bills which after ten years must have been the equivalent of Peru's gross domestic product. This was one fight we didn't want to get involved in, especially if it meant we had no legal right to be in the flat. So sadly it was back to the drawing board.

A couple of days of fruitless searching later and we were back in Cen-tral 88, rubbing our feet and reflecting on our experience so far. We had successfully landed, sampled some of the local cuisine, and had done a little exploration. But despite having seen over thirty flats we still hadn't found something that we liked and which we could also afford, at least without sending Larry to work in the local factories. Even when we started to allow our requirement list to dwindle we were still unable to unearth somewhere that was both affordable and larger than a tea chest, an important consideration when trying to raise a family.

The strain was beginning to show.

"It would be a bit humiliating if we came home because we weren't able to find a flat," said Aggie one morning. I fully agreed. We were less than a week in to our new lives and we were already finding that Hong Kong wouldn't be quite as easy as we had hoped.

SIX

....

A ggie was up and out to work nice and early, leaving Larry and I to our own devices. His particular device that morning was sleep, so I took the opportunity of ten minutes sitting down with the newspaper. Aside from the standard discussions on pop stars, Beijing's views on the world, and nimby-esque complaints on every single proposed development, today's edition of the South China Morning Post revealed yet more news about a story that had gripped the public for over a decade.

Hong Kong is not an equal place. In fact it rates an astonishing eleventh in one global measure of worst income inequality, beaten only by paradigms of corruption like Haiti and the Central African Republic. Although the real, fly-blown, bone-crushing poverty that blights other parts of the world doesn't really exist here, there are people living hard lives with very little money at all. It is common, for example, to see elderly women pushing rubbish carts up and down the slopes of Central, in charge of loads that probably wouldn't be given to healthy young lads in the West. There are also the cage dwellers. Whilst many families are forced to live in tiny flats—a friend of mine was living with his brother and parents in an apartment measuring five hundred square feet, and he considered himself middle class in terms of earning power—some people are so destitute that they have to live in actual cages, piled on top of each other, no more than sixteen square feet in size. Bed bugs eat them alive, there is no kitchen, and they wash their clothes in a bucket. This truly is primitive living, and right in the midst of one of the world's wealthiest cities. Thankfully it appears that these insults to habitation, originally aimed at mainly male migrant workers from Mainland China, are decreasing in prevalence, but their abolition and the provision of humane housing for all cannot come soon enough.

At the other end of the income scale are those with absolutely incredible amounts of money. Hong Kong has, for example, the most Rolls-Royce per capita, the most Mercedes outside of Germany, and the most millionaires: two hundred and twelve thousand in 2012, and the most in the world for its size.

Yet while Hong Kong has plenty of millionaires, it is the number of billionaires that catches the eye. Although the exact figure fluctuates every year as their fortunes wax and wane, it is still more than the whole of Africa combined. There is serious money here.

Of these, some of the best-known were the Wangs. Teddy and Nina—once Asia's richest woman—were refugees from the communist takeover of Shanghai in 1949. They brought with them the keys to what would become one of Hong Kong's wealthiest companies, Chinachem. Whilst not in the same loony category as Howard Hughes, they were both still a bit different from the normal. Nina, even as an old woman, liked to dress as a schoolgirl, with double pigtails and short skirts, and went by the name of 'Little Sweetie'. They also took parsimony to a new level, taking dinner guests to McDonalds, and generally refusing to pay the full price for anything. Rarely has the motto 'save the pennies and the pounds will look after themselves' been executed with such intent.

While thrift may not be the worst sin to commit, it can lead to a few problems down the way. Teddy Wang, for example, refused to employ personal security. Now it's never good, if you're a wildly wealthy tycoon who finds himself horrendously unpopular thanks to refusing to pay the full amount owed to suppliers, colleagues, and so on, to put your safety in the hands of blind optimism rather than hiring a couple of hard men to watch your back. This was especially true as Teddy had already been kidnapped once before, back in 1983. He was only freed after an $11 million ransom was paid, and was eventually found in an iron box by the side of the road.

Refusing to learn this lesson on security requirements became more of an issue when he was kidnapped again on 10 April 1990. This time there was no release, and he was most likely tossed, bound and gagged, into the South China Sea, even though part of another ransom had been delivered. They never did find the body. This though was just the start of the story, or at least the story that interested the public most, because it involved money, charlatans, and intrigue.

Not the biggest fans of engaging lawyers, neither Teddy nor Nina had bothered to pay solicitors' fees to make their wills, which meant that a whole heap of trouble erupted that made British court disputes look like a minor chafing in comparison. Because of the apathetic way that the couple went about recording their wills on random bits of paper, a whole host of contested documents started appearing, and were all keenly argued over.

The first dispute was between Nina and Teddy's father, which was eventually settled in her favour after years of court cases. The next battle came about when Nina died a few years later, and somewhat implausibly involved a short, round-headed fortune teller/feng shui master called Tony Chan.

Feng shui, or the practice of positioning objects and buildings in harmony so as to bring good luck, is wildly popular in Hong Kong. It is taken into account in everything from deciding how to lay out a room, to the design of the largest structures. As part of its feng shui, HSBC has two lions outside its Des Voeux Road headquarters; luck-seeking strangers will often rub their paws and noses raw hoping that some of the bank's good fortune will be absorbed. Less well-known is that on HSBC's roof are two metal rods, also installed thanks to feng shui, to ward off the 'negative energy' radiating from the angular outline of next door's Bank of China tower, a zigzag style building constructed at the end of British rule which some people thought resembled a glass tower with a couple of thunderbolts strapped on. Ironically the Bank of China building didn't take feng shui into account when it was on the drawing board, which caused considerable consternation amongst its neighbours. Apart from the HSBC rods, it was said that the Chief Executive of Hong Kong didn't live in the old Governor's mansion because the Bank of China tower reflected bad feng shui onto the residence.

With all this harmonisation, it isn't surprising that feng shui practitioners are in high demand, and many have become astonishingly wealthy. In past years one of the richest was Tony Chan, who, despite being a millionaire many times over, wanted more; such was his obsession with money that he even named his child 'Wealthee Chan'. His drive for more made him somewhat dubiously claim that his feng shui advisory relationship with Nina had strayed into the romantic, and as a result she had abandoned all reason and left her entire estate to him rather than her charitable trust. It wasn't a total surprise when the judge dismissed his evidence as "untruthful, unreliable and lacking in credibility", and the will he presented as Nina's was declared a forgery. A twelve-year stint inside was Tony's reward.

If I was going to be joining the Wangs in the Billionaire Club I was first going to need some income. I did toy with the idea of setting up my own company, but was dissuaded by a random man I met who, based on his own hard-gained experience, reckoned that at least three years were needed in Asia to understand the ways of business here. As he was two years into running his own communications practice and still earning a pittance, this seemed like sensible logic, so I headed to see some recruiters instead.

For my first head-hunter interview I made the extraordinary decision of walking there. It was thirty degrees, the air was intensely moist, and I was wearing a thick grey suit, so instead of the exercise clearing my head, I arrived thoroughly flustered. My interviewer, a young Welshman who appeared to never have done anything in Hong Kong apart from work, was at least highly knowledgeable about the local job market. With an unemployment rate of between three and four percent—most of whom, he reckoned, were never going to work thanks to ailments or attitude— there were plenty of roles to go around. The problem was that most of the roles were finance related. One of the most popular job sites for foreigners, Asiaxpat, had around two thousand positions listed on it of which over half were accounting or banking, neither of which were suitable for me. Nor were 'night legal secretary', 'blow dry bar beauty care assistant', or 'door closer design engineer'. I had a feeling it was going to be a long search, but the Welshman was optimistic.

"Be patient, something will happen."

That of course was easy for him to say, although looking back it was entirely correct. Yet at the time, after half a dozen similar meetings, and with nothing even remotely suitable rearing its head, I did start to feel a touch of pressure. I had never had a problem finding good roles in the UK, and was puzzled as to why this particular search appeared as if it would take some time. But there was no choice but to keep looking, and besides, there was plenty of family admin still left to do.

SEVEN

....

With Rita not yet delivering the real estate goods it was time to try a new tack. Aggie had already started searching independently to increase the likelihood of finding somewhere, and I was investigating other options too. When a friend of a friend invited me to lunch, I thought I would take the opportunity to ask for some tips on how to do things differently. Alex, the friend, had been here a while and would no doubt have a good few contacts that we could use.

With long blonde hair swept back from his forehead, a thick nose, and steel-rimmed glasses, Alex looked more like a German academic than the English extreme-marathon runner he was. He had invited me to the China Tee Club, a restaurant resembling a film set from 1930s Shanghai. Slow-moving fans rasped above the tiled floors, blowing the leaves of the forest of ferns that lined the walls, and ruffling the hair of the mixed Chinese and expat diners relaxing in black wooden chairs. Soulful, mournful jazz layered the air from high-placed speakers. Its atmosphere was a port of calm amidst the roar of Central outside.

After a while catching up over our shared acquaintances and sampling the Hainanese chicken—a greasy dish that people seem to really dig here, for some decidedly unknown reason—I was about to raise our housing plight when the phone rang. It was Aggie with some good news. She had just been to see a flat and had liked it so much she'd put an offer in there and then, and it had been accepted. We'd be moving to a small three-bedroom flat in the Midlevels part of town within a few days.

Such was the relief that I would have bought a large bottle of champagne if Alex had been drinking, but as it was I settled for another green tea. When I explained where we would be living it turned out that we would be neighbours, separated by only seven floors. This was exciting news, for not only had we found somewhere to live, thus relieving us of an enormous weight of stress, we would have a ready-made social life there too.

Alex was enthusiastic about the Grand Panorama estate, the name of our future home.

"It's a great place to live. You have the shuttle bus to take you down to Central—it's only a fifteen minute walk but why bother, to be honest—and there's an OK gym and a pool. It's even got golf simulators if you like that sort of thing, although they look like they use the same graphics as that old movie Tron. One thing though, don't drink the water. They found Legionnaires disease in it last year." So the place had its positives and deadly negatives, and apparently looked like a concrete council estate in Peckham, but it was going to be home and that's all that mattered after the trauma of finding it.

We wouldn't quite believe it though until our furniture had arrived. We had coincidentally timed the first day of our rent to coincide with the arrival of our container from England, fit to burst with most of the contents of our former, non-expat lives—assuming of course that it would turn up when it was meant to. An hour after it was meant to have arrived we were feeling a bit anxious. Larry was crawling around the wooden floors of our empty new place, poking his nose into the barren cupboards and generally hollering around, but his parents were sitting glumly in the corner.

I briefly worried that our stuff had been washed overboard, but, as became apparent, this was highly unlikely. I know this because I was sufficiently bored to look up the probability while I waited. Apparently only around ten thousand containers were lost each year, out of around two hundred million container journeys in the same period—so about the same odds as an American dying in a plane crash. It was far more likely the removal men were just stuck in traffic, which, of course, they were.

They arrived with a great fanfare of trolleys and bubblewrap and a work ethic bordering on the manic. The leader of the gang was, in true removal style the world over, called Bob, and seemed to be either quite deaf or just fond of shouting.

"YOU WANT CHAIR HERE? HERE? HERE? HERE? HERE?" he bellowed, pointing at every possible place the sofa could go. Er, there was just fine, thank you.

"OR HERE?" Despite the endless variations on a theme our possessions were very quickly unpacked, and by five in the afternoon Bob and the rest had left.

We sat on our sofa, which, amazingly, was actually not quite where we had wanted it, and looked at the full bookshelves and the photos neatly arranged on them. Our possessions looked stunned, as if they had been tranquilised in London and woken up in a semi-tropical funk. Still, they weren't as out of place as our rattan chairs back in Leicestershire.

There was a knock at the door; I nudged Aggie from our daze and she went to answer. Stood before her was a middle-aged Chinese woman in a flowing blue dress, her hair in a jagged bob and bedecked in multi-coloured jewels. She held out her hands and grasped Aggie by the shoulders.

"Welcome! We are so glad to have new neighbours. Oh my God, the previous guys were so awful!" The deep, honeyed accent was half way between Brooklyn and Hong Kong, and the enthusiasm all theatre. Aggie looked slightly askance, and Larry, who was playing on the floor next to the entrance, turned his head to see what the commotion was.

"Oh my God I see you have a little one. Well, I can be his Hong Kong Grandma! Do you have everything you need? Tea, coffee? Do you want me to cook you something? You must come over and meet Guy.

He's resting right now but would love to meet you. How were the movers?"

We had no choice but to invite Vivian in, and she plonked herself down without pausing for air. She had a warmth that radiated like a coke fire and we sat talking for what seemed like forever—well, for at least the duration of two mugs of tea.

She was, like Little Sweetie, originally from Shanghai and a refugee from the communists; it certainly seemed that back then anyone that had any money, or the means, to get out of the Mainland in 1949 did so, and many came to Hong Kong.

"Oh my God when I first came here it seemed like such a backwater. I remember asking Mom where all the escalators were, but Hong Kong didn't have any back then. Shanghai was much wealthier." It wasn't just Shanghai that she knew about. Within half an hour we had become familiar with every piece of available knowledge and gossip about our new block: who worked where, which couples had the best behaved children, and what the stay at home wife of so-and-so really did with her time. Back home we wouldn't have been much interested in the local scandals, given the lack of interaction that Londoners on the whole have with their neighbours, but here it was like a window on a new world, and an entertaining window at that.

Sadly Larry was soon in need of a bath and bed, so Vivian left us with promises of imminent visits.

"Oh honey, I've got so much more to tell you about living here. And just wait till you taste my cookies." We really had landed on our feet if all our neighbours were as kind as this.

After a tepid night's sleep—we still had no curtains up—we decided to go exploring our new neighbourhood. According to local historian Jason Wordie, until the 1950s the Midlevels was an area thick with plush houses and terraced gardens overlooking the sea. The China-born author Han Suyin described the night view of harbour lights and neon as being like the 'hoard of a jewel thief'. The most magnificent of these houses was the aptly named Marble Hall. It was sixty thousand square feet of mansion lined with thick green vein marble and, so it was said, an equal to many a European stately home, a suitable statement of success for its owner.

Of all the people that could have been said to have made Hong Kong the thriving merchant city it is today the builder of Marble Hall, Sir Catchick Paul Chater, is one of the most significant. In fact, on his death in 1926, the South China Morning Post reported that 'A biography of Sir Paul Chater would be a history of Hong Kong.' He had a thick, square, and bald head, with a bristling white, comb-like moustache, and looked like the kind of man that would have been determined to get his own way.

Like so many successful men and women he suffered from a disturbed childhood. Born in Calcutta to Armenian parents, he was an orphan by the time he was seven, but came to Hong Kong as a highly driven and obviously capable teenager. Starting off as a junior bank assistant, he soon resigned to go solo, and, based on some nifty gold and land trading, was a millionaire by the time he was thirty. He was obviously a man who wasn't constricted by a lack of ambition, helping to found many Hong Kong companies which are leaders even today: Hongkong Telephone, Dairy Farm, Hongkong Land, even a ferry service. It was Sir Paul too that started the first large-scale reclamation of the colony, a massive scheme two miles long and two hundred and fifty feet wide. He even performed some of the soundings for it himself, taking depth readings at night from his little boat, or 'sampan' as they were called here. He also took the credit for bringing electricity to the colony, buying a graveyard in Wanchai to install a power station. Not content with dominating the business world, he managed to become a highly successful horse breeder and played cricket in the colony's first eleven.

Clearly Sir Paul was not a man to do things by halves. It made sense therefore that Marble Hall was the most opulent house in the colony, its form surpassed only by its contents; a priceless collection of Chinese glass and antiques. Considering that the average price of a flat in Mid-levels was around $2,000 per square foot, this would have made Marble Hall worth around £100 million if it were still standing today.

But sadly, like so much of the past here, it has been swept away. All the old mansions have been sold off for development, those cosy homes replaced by huge, non-descript concrete towers that are the Dementors of architecture. Apparently some old China hands remember the Mid-levels having one or two mansions remaining until the 1970s, but by then they were the last old soldiers, soon to be totally replaced—and indeed forgotten—by the new generation.

For now, despite the Midlevels looking like a slightly more colourful version of East Berlin circa 1970, we were happy with our new neighbourhood. The large houses may have gone, but at least we could buy groceries, visit a local restaurant, or, most importantly, frequent the bars of Soho—a prime nightlife area five minutes' walk downhill from our flat. It was also full of history, as reflected in the street names. Rednaxela Terrace (which if you notice is 'Alexander' spelt backwards) and Chico Terrace, both originally home to the large Portuguese community that once lived in Hong Kong. Neighbouring Shelley Street was named for an early colonial administrator who was renowned for his uselessness and, as one governor disapproving described, for being "dissipated, negligent, unreliable and in debt." Convenience, beer, and history made sure that this was going to be a great place to live.

EIGHT

....

I t was intriguing to think that Hong Kong was, like an extra child, a bit of an accident. There was no great British plan to capture the island, and certainly no Machiavellian strategy to take the pearl of the orient away from a weak China and turn it into a global trading hub. For a start, Hong Kong wasn't even on most maps at the time, being almost uninhabited, and second there were far better targets for Britain elsewhere in China, if indeed there was any desire to conquer somewhere in the first place.

Instead, Hong Kong came into being as the fortunate by-product of a series of events, all initiated by perhaps the most unsuitable trade envoy in history.

In 1833 Lord Palmerston, the Foreign Secretary, thought it prudent to appoint a Chief Superintendent of Trade to oversee the expanding business then being conducted by British merchants in and around the southern Chinese city of Canton, now Guangzhou, and in particular act as a liaison with the Chinese Emperor's appointee there. It was to be a friendly mission, and the Superintendent was ordered "to cautiously abstain from all unnecessary use of menacing language...to study by all practicable methods to maintain the good and friendly understanding, and to ensure that all British subjects understood their duty to obey the laws and usages of the Chinese Empire."

Unfortunately, the man chosen for the task was absolutely and utterly unsuited to it, other than that he happened to have a few political pals. Lord William Napier had a distinct lack of experience in both trade and diplomacy—two pretty key skills, you might think—and was instead best-known for the stunningly irrelevant A Treatise on Practical Store farming as applicable to the Mountainous Region of Ettrick Forest and the Pastoral District of Scotland in General.

With a touch of luck and a warm character, someone like Lord Napier could have made a successful go of it. Unfortunately, Lord Napier had the personality of an ass. He was, by all accounts, difficult, awkward, opinionated, and to cap it all he was ginger. This, according to a contemporary, was to the Chinese 'a particular and diabolical abomination.' The Morning Post newspaper went so far as to note that Lord Napier knew "as much of the port of Canton, and the very difficult duties to be performed there, as an orang-utang."

Not one to blanch in the face of total unsuitability, Lord Napier instead relied on overbearing confidence, shouting, and an irresistible desire to do something when doing nothing was the best option. All three traits were soon put to use, and in no time at all he had managed to bluster his way through so many local rules and regulations that he had alienated both the local Chinese authorities and the British traders that he had come to support. All this culminated in him ordering two Royal Navy frigates up the Pearl River, where the Chinese promptly sealed them in with the help of some sunken barges across the river mouth, thus making the ships totally redundant. Napier had no choice but to retreat back to the Portuguese colony of Macao through the gauntlet of Chinese jeering. Within five weeks he was dead, struck down by disease and the deadly effects of hubris.

Lord Napier did have one useful legacy, above and beyond strained diplomatic relations. It was he who first suggested using the island of Hong Kong as a British trading post, an idea that was taken up by the one person that could be said to have birthed Hong Kong.

Unlike Sir Stamford Raffles in Singapore, or George Washington in the US, Hong Kong has no publicly-acknowledged Founding Father to honour with tea towels or jelly moulds. But there is one man that could fill that role, albeit not by design. Captain Charles Elliot, a German-born Royal Navy officer with a beard like a rhododendron bush, was a successor to Lord Napier as a Chief Superintendent of Trade. His position meant that following Britain's victory in the First Opium War, he was able to dictate the terms of peace with the Chinese. The local merchants and Britain in general were thinking of a great prize, a piece of land—maybe Taiwan—that could be held as a way of forcing China to better trade terms. It was trade, not territory, that Britain wanted at this point.

Charles Elliot hadn't settled on which territory to demand as the spoils of war, as indicated by the fact that the treaty document was blank after the words "the cessation of the islands of..." For some reason, never fully explained, Elliot struck out the 's' on islands and added the words 'Hong Kong' after it. He was perhaps aware of the recommendation of Lord Napier—although why anyone would have thought it a good idea to listen to him isn't clear—or just believed that, as a naval man, Victoria Harbour was too good a natural port and shelter from typhoons to ignore.

Whatever the reason, the result was that Britain now owned the obscure, barren, and almost uninhabited island of Hong Kong for ever more. The merchants were spitting, and the government wasn't best pleased either; Elliot was soon sacked and sent back home in disgrace. His name did live on for a few years in the form of a street name above Central, but even this legacy was expunged from the record when Elliot's Vale was renamed Gleanealy. Considering the number of nobodies with roads named after them in Hong Kong, this was some snub.

At least it can be said that Captain Elliot would surely have liked the supremely pleasant Gleanealy, even without his name attached. About a ten minute walk from our flat, it was a tree-lined path that lead from the Midlevels down into Central, and a good place to start a run. I was using my enforced time off to get fitter, which had the added benefit of letting me get to know the Midlevels a bit better. There were numerous paths and trails to follow, but my favourite was Bowen Road.

It was apt that this long, sinewy track should be named after someone that the Australian Dictionary of Biography had described as "self-opinionated, obstinate, and long-winded." Sir George Bowen, a late nineteenth-century governor, was a man that almost everyone in Hong Kong disliked. One local paper went so far as to claim that "Great Britain's supremacy could not long be maintained if there were many responsible officers in the service of the Crown of the calibre of Sir George Bowen," and when he left, his tour of duty cut short due to 'ill health', there was no one to see him off. As a local merchant put it, "No arrangements were being made for any farewell entertainment, and he sent for Mr Ryrie and asked him to organise a demonstration of some kind, but that gentleman declined." Cocking a snook at a departing worthy seemed to be quite the done thing in those early years.

Still, like Captain Elliot, he left behind a nice place to run. Hedged by trees, ferns, and houses so nouveau that they would have looked at home in Dubai, Bowen Road followed the contour of the mountain that dominated Hong Kong, the Peak, and so was possibly the only stretch of flat ground in this part of town. It was a most agreeable place to spend an hour or so, with many a diverting sight.

At the start of Bowen Road, I soon noticed, was a remarkable little building called Mother's Choice. This was, in the parlance of old, an orphanage. According to the South China Morning Post, only around one hundred and twenty children were adopted in Hong Kong each year, and most of these were from either Mother's Choice or one of its affiliates. Occasionally I would run past the white, school-like building that lay just below street level in time to see the babies being laid out for an outdoor sleep. With a desire to do something well-intentioned with our time we enquired about volunteering there, but were told that there was a waiting list, six months long, just to be able to help out.

If giving them a hand was such a popular thing to do, then why weren't more children adopted? Part of it, so I read, was because local culture frowned on adoption, although I had never asked a Chinese person to see if this was just lazy journalism. At least there was a place for the discarded to be cared for; it is said that in the old days of Hong Kong unwanted babies—especially girls—were often left to die.

Like many a path here, Bowen Road also had a number of outdoor playgrounds. Hong Kong was littered with these, for both young and old, and it could at first be difficult to tell the difference; both had brightly coloured machines and rubber floor mats. One morning I was up and out early, and perturbed to discover a half-dozen middle-aged women at the kiddies' playground brandishing swords—and I mean swords: two-foot-long pieces of sharp metal with pronounced pokey ends that wouldn't half have smarted if they had come too close. I was half way to calling the police when I realised that they were all moving in time to each other, performing some kind of jerky tai chi that made them look like they were being goosed by invisible strangers. I quickly ran off.

Tai chi was certainly something that I didn't understand. If I was awake early enough I would see hundreds if not thousands of men and woman slowly waving their arms and legs around in the street, and not all of them were armed. One of the key attractions for us being here was to learn about the Chinese culture, but this was a part of it that I just didn't get—yet. It was still fascinating to watch though, and an insight into the local culture which was becoming more and more interesting the deeper we explored it.

There was only so much exploration of the local Chinese culture that I could do on Hong Kong Island, which was in many ways a goldfish bowl of internationalism with its own unique subculture. So, a few weeks into our move, I decided to head up north to the New Territories and see a different side of Hong Kong.

I settled on the new town of Shatin, it being home of a racecourse and also blessed with a faintly amusing name. I imagined a smaller version of Milton Keynes, but with fewer roundabouts, fewer chavs, and definitely fewer crowds, and was looking forward to a pavement we could walk along at a normal pace—with even a bit of space around me.

Another reason for going was that I had, at some networking event or another, met one of the men responsible for designing Shatin, and he had suggested a trip to see this nouveau part of the SAR. Richard Garrett may not have been well-known, but he had probably a greater physical legacy here than any other person in the territory; he was the man who had designed most of Hong Kong's infrastructure, from the tunnels to the sewers. He even came up with the shape of all the thousands of road sign gantries here. On top of it all, he also helped bring to life the Mid-levels escalator, which is literally an outdoors escalator that connects Central with the slopes above and is used by tens of thousands of commuters each day. Given the heat and humidity this must be one of the most welcome infrastructure projects of all time. Not bad for an unassuming man who originally came out to Hong Kong 'for something to do.' Garrett, like Allan Zeman, was definitely a man who showed just how much opportunity lay in Hong Kong if you were willing and able to pursue it.

Larry and I were going to take the MTR to Shatin. I hadn't yet spent much time on the underground lines; its workings were a mystery to me, and for some reason I had no desire to demystify myself. Maybe it was the fear of getting lost, maybe it was the complication of buying a ticket, or maybe it was not being arsed to carry Larry's buggy down the escalator-free stairwells.

My preferred yet decadent mode of transport was instead the taxi, which was a snip at two pounds a ride. Yet these taxi fares, though remarkably cheap, were starting to mount up. Back in London I was a real bus aficionado, even the night bus; that cold, dangerous hideout of the morally infirm. But the thought of trying to get Larry, pushchair, and accompanying bags onto a double-decker more tightly packed than the

Black Hole of Calcutta seemed too much of a challenge even for me, and especially for the sake of a pittance saving per journey.

Another option was the green Toyota minibuses that stormed up and down the streets, and which you could hail much like a cab. Like a taxi, their drivers—or 'captains' as they jauntily called themselves—made the vehicles feel like an extension of themselves, with their newspapers and packed lunch and spare clothes and odds and ends piled up around their seats (or helms, if you prefer). The way they worked was for the passengers to shout a warning that they wanted to alight. I tried this once in English and no stop was made, so naturally assumed that I had to communicate with the skipper in Cantonese. I therefore made a concerted effort to memorise a number of useful phrases like 'I want to get off at the next stop', but the only one I could ever remember was to ask him to 'let me out at the bridge'. This had the unfortunate effect of reducing my routes to those criss-crossed by flyovers, which rather inconveniently didn't include my home.

A major downside of the minibuses, apart from my inability to stop where I wanted, was that they were even more child unfriendly than the big buses for getting pushchairs in and out and, frankly, the driving was actually dangerous. My first trip in one, on my own thank goodness, was memorable for the driver managing to touch the curb with the back left wheel whilst travelling at speed around a sharp, sloping corner. The two seconds we were on two wheels felt very long indeed.

There was of course always the option of walking. The trouble with this was the climate, as I had found out on my walk to my first interview. When it rained it was impossible to be outside and not become totally soaked, down to even your underwear, in a matter of seconds. But what was worse was the combination of heat and humidity that wracked the streets for much of the year; weather that reduced suits to a dripping jelly and turned shirts see-through, which was not a good look on most. Luckily the urban planners of Hong Kong were obviously highly aware of the horrors of prolonged ambulation in the humid heat. They had after all built the Midlevels escalator. In addition they had also managed to connect vast swathes of the city with indoor corridors that kept the pedestrian in luxurious air-conditioning, and not just on the ground floor, but often many storeys up. The noticeable thing about this network was that many of these routes went straight through banks, office buildings, and other institutions that in other countries would have strongly objected to random strangers passing through. Yet here somehow it worked, even if the odd tourist accidentally found his way into a company's boardroom.

But in order to get to Shatin I had to take the plunge and use the MTR. Now, whereas London's Underground map was almost bucolic with names like Southfields, Covent Garden, or even Grange Hill, Hong Kong's rail planners had showed very little imagination in naming most of the stations, at least if you didn't speak Cantonese. 'Mass Transit Railway' was, for a start, hardly in the same poetic league as the 'Tube', and the station names took this functional descriptiveness even further. 'Central' was probably the most boring name, but the excitement was hardly raised by such titles as 'Causeway Bay', 'University', or my personal favourite, 'City One'. The trouble with the local names was that they all sounded quite similar to the uninitiated. Tai Wo and Tai Po were happily enough on the same line—indeed, were next to each other—but Tai Wo Hau was miles away, and Tai Koo was even further. Making sure I was exactly accurate with the destination name was a lesson quickly learned.

Anyway, I dragged Larry's buggy down the stairs and into the den of the commuter. Around five million people used the MTR each day, and it showed. The carriages were super-packed, and in a probably not unrelated manner there were plenty of signs imploring people to report sexual assault, aka fondling. This wasn't the 1970s Sid James type, where a small bald man squeezed a woman's breasts whilst shouting "Parp, parp!" It was instead more akin to the story of the man that rode up and down the MTR escalator taking photos up the skirts of unwilling women. Still, it wasn't anywhere near as bad as Japan, where they are forced to have women-only carriages.

Arriving at last in Shatin we went straight into a nice air-conditioned mall, and found that far from the town being a less crowded place, we were still surrounded by what seemed to be millions of people. I shouldn't have been surprised given Hong Kong's population density, which is twenty-two times that of the UK and a crowd-busting three thousand, two hundred and thirteen times that of Australia. No wonder Shatin was full; everywhere in Hong Kong was.

Larry and I decided to get some lunch, but all those people had to eat somewhere, and they had decided to do it at exactly the same time we had. We wandered around for a while, but all the food courts had queues longer than a Harry Potter book launch. Eventually we did find a place that was quite empty, a French-themed sandwich shop. There were tastier treats floating in Victoria Harbour, but we were hungry and it was time to stop.

Refuelled, our next challenge was to go to the park—well, a stretch of grass with a bench on it—that we had glimpsed through a window. We walked around looking for the obvious exit, but found nothing. We tried again on a different floor, but just ended up passing more and more stores without finding anything remotely like a sign or a map. It did give us the chance to see some interesting shops, and realise just how much money there must be in Hong Kong for there to be about a million Cartier shops in one mall in one new town, but still we couldn't find an exit. It reminded me of the scene in European Vacation when Chevy Chase and family just couldn't "get off the damned roundabout. Look there's Big Ben kids, and Parliament, again." After an hour and a half of failed attempts and a bucketful of approaches to blank-looking sales assistants, we gave up and returned to the station, which was the only thing signed. What a day. But at least we understood Hong Kong life a bit better.

NINE

....

O n a positive note, our social life, which to this point had shown less life than a frog in a school dissection class, was beginning to stir. For a start there was Alex and his wife Emily living below us, although we hadn't actually seen them yet apart from an initial welcome-to-Grand-Panorama cup of tea. Then there was Tom.

One night, as is often the way in Hong Kong as people seek out new friends, we found ourselves invited to join a group of strangers at a Manchurian restaurant. Now this was not a cuisine that I actually knew about, let alone had tasted before, but it was tasty fare. Our host was someone I had met briefly back in the UK at a stag do, and who had arrived in Hong Kong a short while before us. A stocky, square-jawed country type from the West of England, Tom was good fun and single, and therefore keen on a drink or two at night.

"Don't worry, I'll show you the good bars," he had promised, and he didn't let us down.

First though we had to deal with the rat. Our weighty meal of roast lamb, spicy dumplings, and Tsingtao beer was interrupted by the sight of a large black rodent scurrying unhurriedly across the floor. None of the other guests seemed to notice but the women on our table certainly did. A heady scream brought a waitress over, but rather than acquiesce to our demands on a discount to the bill that was about to arrive, she dismissed the rat as "a neighbour from next door" before flouting off to make us pay full whack. A standoff only served to produce a half-hour delay to the rest of our night, so realising there was not much more to do, we shrugged our shoulders and went looking for a beer.

Tom took us into the thick of late night drinking. We were very much looking forward to a night allowing the recently started Tessie to take the strain, so were determined that wherever we went we would enjoy. I was hoping that we would be going to LKF, where my cousin had introduced me to many a new night-time concept, and so was delighted when Tom took us down a busy Wyndham Street, down some black stairs, and onto the familiar cobbles I had known so well. Yet sadly it was not as I remembered at all. For some reason LKF was undergoing a whole-scale renovation, and most of the bars I remembered from old had closed. Yeltsin's for one was no longer there. This was probably because no one gave a damn about the old Soviet Union any more, although it could just have been that, like most of the bar turnover, its owners had declined to accept the ever-rising rent increases and passed the baton to someone with deeper pockets.

That said, we were still spoilt for choice. You could find a Happy Hour just about any hour, and every type of cuisine was available, from Turkish to Tartar to Thai. The crowd was completely multicultural, with a mix of tanned expats, holidaymakers, and local Chinese all just enjoying not being at work. And despite the vast quantities of booze being quaffed, the atmosphere felt about as threatening as a church choir.

After checking out a couple of anonymous pubs we headed to one down a small side street that looked a little hedonistic, and which was also a hundred percent packed.

"Wait here," said Tom, and shot inside. A couple of minutes later he appeared accompanied by the proprietress, a middle-aged Chinese woman with short, neat hair, thick milk-bottle glasses, and thin lips that were very much on the verge of a sneer.

She took a careful look at our group before announcing, with a flick of her hand, that we would soon have a table. Tom was obviously someone useful to know when looking for a place to party. He'd only been in Hong Kong a few weeks longer than us but was already years ahead in his social life.

The rest of the night was spent in abject merriment, getting to know Tom and his pals better and celebrating the feeling of being able to party with people who were great company. But a few hours later the highlife began to take a toll after months of sleepless nights and so we sauntered home, leaving Tom chatting up a girl whose top half was clad only in a bra made of real coconuts. Hong Kong was definitely a lively place.

Sadly I was not going to be able to spend all my non-working time at the pub. The other extreme, a life dedicated to CV submission and interview practise, was even less attractive. I was in need of a hobby.

For some masochistic reason I chose to fill this void with Mandarin lessons. Despite my university debacle I thought there was unfinished business with getting to grips with the language. This would be an academic challenge, for sure; a recent study had calculated that, for an English speaker, learning to speak Chinese was twenty percent more difficult than learning to speak French, and learning to write Chinese was five hundred percent harder. But I had to do something with my time, so, I thought, why not?

I chose the Hong Kong Chinese Language School at random. It was on the second floor of a rickety old high-rise with a rickety old lift and an even more rickety old concierge, with cheeks like leather and a permanently confused expression—both of which indicated far too long in the sun. After a quick introductory chat with Jonathan the manager—and given his halitosis, thank goodness it was quick—I was shown into a classroom to meet my teacher. Aged twenty-three, with a curt black bob and a face fresh from a music video, New Moon was very different from the old codgers that I'd normally had as teachers at school. A glamorous teacher back in Leicestershire was someone who washed her hair every day and wore make-up.

Despite her looks, New Moon soon revealed herself to be no light touch. Any mistake I made in pronunciation, and there were very, very many, I assure you, was quickly picked up with a barked "No. Say it again. You must improve." I was grateful that she didn't carry a sharp-edged ruler, but at least I was learning quickly.

There was much more to learn from her than just the language. I was particularly interested in the nuances of writing in characters, like how did you sign your name? ("Most Hong Kongers sign in English," she explained in a why-did-you-ask-such-an-obtuse-question kind of manner), and how did you type or send text messages? ("By using predictive text, obviously.")

She also educated me on important cultural elements, such as the public holidays, which, apart from the Christian ones left over from the British, generally had a link to China's past. September ended with our first public holiday, a highlight of the celestial calendar known as the Mid-Autumn Festival. This is one of the most famous and most cele-brated holidays; a sort of Harvest Festival, Thanksgiving, and fertility rite rolled into one. So ingrained was it in the national psyche that decades of repression on the Mainland couldn't wipe it from the collective memory, and in 2008 the Communist Party of China actually re-established it as a national holiday. Traditionally families would come together to bring in the crops, give thanks for the bounty, and then try and pair off members of their family to eligible partners. As our neighbour Vivian told us, it was still apparently the custom in certain parts of China for matchmak-ing dances to be held at this time for single men and women.

Here in Hong Kong the most conspicuous part of the festival is not romance, but food. Now boiled egg and black sesame paste baked into a pie is not to everyone's taste unless, of course, you are Chinese. Mooncakes, as these quizzical delicacies are known, are to the Mid-Autumn Festival what Brussels sprouts are to Christmas lunches; everyone eats them, either for pleasure or from guilt. This included us, who were determined to try them no matter how unappetising they seemed. At first the mix of sweet sesame seed paste and hard-boiled egg didn't seem so bad, but soon my taste buds put two and two together and didn't like the answer. These were probably the only cakes that weren't for me.

Happily the Festival was more than just novel culinary concoctions. There were numerous celebrations across the territory, like the fire dragon of Tai Hang. Located just at the edge of Causeway Bay, on the north side of Hong Kong Island, this was a small village which had had quite a run of bad luck a hundred years before. First a typhoon came and wrought havoc, and no sooner had the wind died down than a plague struck. Then, as legend would have it, a python came along and ate all their livestock. Whereas not many Westerners would have responded to these catastrophes by building a two hundred and twenty-foot-long fiery dragon from straw, this is what the villagers did, and much to their relief and, I daresay, amazement, the plague ceased. Ever since the locals have replicated the ceremony, watched by the thousands who make their way to Tai Hang to see the dragon dance and drench the air with smoke.

For many people though, the simplest traditions were the most practical to follow. With it being a lunar festival, it was apparently a very popular activity to climb high to get a better look at the moon. As the most easily accessible altitude on the island was the Peak we headed upwards to join the thousands of others that had also made the trek. Little children swarmed around despite the late hour, holding a variety of multi-coloured lanterns shaped as fish, rabbits, dragons, or just glowing red balls. It was a supremely jolly atmosphere. As we looked over the glinting city, surrounded by the satisfied chomping of Mooncakes and families chatting and laughing together, we felt very much settled. We had after all found somewhere to live, sorted out our childcare, and even started our social lives. Things were going very well indeed.

TEN

....

I
t wasn't just the Mid-Autumn Festival that revolved around food; it was becoming increasingly clear that food was the bedrock, the lynchpin, and the defining ingredient of Hong Kong's culture. As the critic A. A. Gill once said of the local cooking, "Its variety, quality, ingenuity and expense, its atavistic extraction, collection, preparation and consumption is metaphorically, allegorically, philosophically, literally gobsmacking." Hong Kong boasts one of the world's highest per-capita concentrations of cafés and restaurants, with one restaurant for every six hundred people, where forty percent of the population has a job connected to restaurants or hotels, and where eating out is so common that restaurants make their money from food not drink. It also chomps its way through more pork per person than anywhere else on the planet, and has more three-star Michelin restaurants than the UK. Food is important.

Someone that was going to enjoy this aspect of Hong Kong was our first visitor. Paul, a former housemate from university and an enthusiastic gastrophile, had decided to take advantage of our move and come explore Hong Kong. Notwithstanding a trip to Ocean Park, Hong Kong's superior version of Disney World, his trip revolved around eating. Much of our time was spent sampling a particular favourite from my first visit, the local speciality of dim sum, which I had first tasted with

Graham at the remnants of one of Hong Kong's finest hotels, now destroyed.

The Repulse Bay, lying in the bay of the same name on the south of Hong Kong Island, was one of the colony's finest hotels right from the time it opened its doors back in the 1920s. Photos of the old place revealed a large matron of a building, homely yet rather stern in an imperial kind of way. She seemed to have had numerous wings, all with colonnaded balconies that reflected the classical style so common in British buildings in this part of the world. Coinciding with a rise in the number of motor cars on the island was good for the hotel, as it allowed the city dwellers an easier and quicker way down out of the urban parts. No doubt the winding night-time road back to Central wiped out a fair number of them after an evening on the pink gins, but the large numbers of businessmen and travellers from across Asia who were discovering the Repulse Bay made sure the hotel was never short of custom.

Sadly Hong Kong and Shanghai Hotels, the owners of the still-standing Peninsula Hotel and possibly of the largest fleet of Rolls-Royces in the territory, demolished the Repulse Bay in the early 1980s, like so many other colonial structures. The reason, as ever in Hong Kong, was to make more money. No matter how many visitors the hotel had they would never be able to compete with selling the land off for flats, which was exactly what happened. Bizarrely, and for an unknown reason, a few years later the company rebuilt part of the hotel. Rumours abounded that the current building was only two-thirds the size of the original, but although it couldn't be that hard to prove, no one seemed to know the truth.

Although the hotel was gone, part of the heritage remained in the form of an atmospheric restaurant, the Verandah. It was here in January 1996 that I first tasted dim sum.

It is not often, after early childhood, that we encounter a totally new type of food that we like enough to become a beloved staple. Yet these wonderful gastronomic encounters do happen. My mother, for example, remembers her first taste of yoghurt on a Reading market stall in the 1960s; it has been an addiction ever since. For me, the first time I encountered those tasty little dumplings is a date my taste buds shan't forget. Originally eaten as just a snack—the name means 'touch the heart' rather than 'fill you up quick'—dim sum has become a staple of Cantonese cooking, especially here in Hong Kong.

Consuming dim sum is much more than just eating; there is etiquette to it too. It may be slight, but it does turn the meal into something more than just stopping hunger. Take for example the tea. Although the waiter will fill up your cup without asking, it is generally customary to pour the tea for your fellow diners yourself, as it is in Britain. A unique twist though is that the tea recipients thank you by tapping their bent index finger if you are single or, if married, tapping two digits, a ritual meant to symbolise bowing.

The practice is said to have been inspired by a certain emperor, who one night decided to go out to eat incognito with some hangers-on. When he poured his courtier some tea, the man wanted to thank his emperor for the privilege of having his cup filled, so tapped on the table so as not to blow his boss' cover. Well, that was the legend. It was far more likely that it had just evolved as a time-saving device; why say "thank you" when you can just tap a little, thus not having to stop eating for even a second? Anyone that had seen a hungry person scoffing dim sum could easily understand this.

The most famous dim sum institution, named Maxim's, was strangely housed in City Hall. It was here that I took Paul to sample the best that Hong Kong had to offer. We arrived early, having heard about the horrendous queues that form after midday, and were shown to a round table covered in a heavily starched ivory cloth. Every minute or so a uniformed woman would come past our table, pushing a clattery old trolley overloaded with dim sum of every type. There were endless plates and baskets of goodies, the extravagant number of courses a novelty to someone only used to starter, main course, and pudding. White buns filled with sickly sweet barbeque pork; prawn balls wrapped in a translucent skin; red roasted pig ribs; lotus leaf envelopes filled with glutinous rice; small squares of fluffy turnip cake; fresh, light spring rolls; salt and pepper squid strips. All were chewed down with an unbecoming greed. Well, nearly all—we avoided the 'Phoenix Claws', aka chicken feet. I had those once in London's Chinatown, and I had no intention of sucking out bones from a glutinous, tasteless mass ever again.

Whereas dim sum was popular with Chinese families for Saturday and Sunday mornings, most expats would enjoy another culinary highlight of Hong Kong: champagne brunch. Every hotel worth its salt, and many a restaurant too, put on a weekend display aimed at stuffing their guests as one would a goose on a foie gras farm; huge displays of meat and drink that would make even the most profligate gourmand blush.

Our first flirtation with this was at the aptly named Jumbo, a floating restaurant just off the south coast of the island by a town named Aberdeen. Now, the concept of yin and yang—in simple terms meaning that opposites only exist in relation to each other—lies at the origin of many branches of Chinese culture and philosophy. It could be said that Hong Kong's Aberdeen was the yin to its Scottish namesake's yang. One was a town full of sports clubs and calamari, one had Irn Bru and deep-fried pizza. One was drenched in sun, one was flooded with fog. One had a drink problem, one had a...wait, they both did. One of the first things we saw when we arrived—at 2.30pm—at the all-you-can-eat-and-drink buffet was a man face down at his table, apparently drowning in his soup. A woman stood over him fanning him with a napkin, but she was hardly a rock of stability herself. The rest of the table, who going by appearances were all Australian second-hand car salesmen, weren't unduly alarmed by the scene.

With Paul in tow we decided on a more dignified eatery: the Intercontinental hotel, across Victoria Harbour in Kowloon. Although there were several tunnels under the water, by far the most civilised way of reaching it was by taking a Star Ferry. This old collection of boats, which looked like small, green and white Mississippi steamers, with wooden slat-seats and chugging diesel engines, were all named after a star of some kind (stars of the celestial kind rather than from the movies). That said, there was, as we discovered by accident when we took a wrong turn to the hotel, an Avenue of Stars. This was a short promenade adjacent to the Harbour that paid homage to over a hundred local actors and actresses. We were sufficiently sheltered from Hong Kong cinema to be only able to recognize more than a handful, but those that we did—Michelle Yeoh, Jackie Chan, Jet Li, Chow Yun-fat, and of course Bruce Lee, who looked threatening even made from brass—were testament in themselves to a highly successful local industry.

We had built up an appetite from our lost wanderings around Kowloon, but not enough for what lay before us. Never before had I seen so much food. It made Jumbo look like Mini Mouse, such was its spread, and Paul, not a man to turn down a challenge or a free feed, looked more excited than I'd seen him in a long time. After about four or five plates I was full, and felt content to sit back and let my stomach focus on its Herculean digestive task. Paul though was only getting started. Alaskan crabs' legs, jumbo prawns, Peking duck, sushi, sashimi, eggs, pork products aplenty, and of course dim sum, all finished off by a sickening choice of desserts. An hour later and Paul was slowly running out of steam. But not the Chinese guy at the next table, who was still going up for more as we wearily headed back across the Harbour, leaving a trail of busted buttons behind us. It's safe to say that Paul left Hong Kong a thoroughly satiated man.

ELEVEN

....

I t wasn't long before we headed back to Kowloon. We had only had a few trips off the island, and so were beginning to feel a little constrained—a not too surprising feeling given that it was only fifty percent larger than Manhattan and barely a fifth the size of the Isle of Wight. It was time to spread our wings once more and get on the sightseeing trail.

Our first stop Kowloon-side (for some reason everything was described as being either Hong Kong-side, meaning on the island, or Kowloon-side, predictably meaning on the Kowloon) was Chungking Mansions, a dilapidated reminder that Hong Kong is not just about rich Chinese and gweilos. Despite looking like a decaying pustule amidst the glitz of à la mode shopping, there is something eye-catching about the place. Each day some four thousand people of over a hundred different nationalities can be found in the seventeen-storey building, some buying goods, others staying in one of the many hostels that occupy its upper floors. Nepali drug addicts, Bangladeshi prostitutes, Turkish restaurateurs, Chinese and Indian hostel owners, Ghanaian traders, and others from every background imaginable, all mixed in a place that has been called the 'most globalised building in the world.' For anyone familiar with London, it feels like Edgware Road, King's Cross, and Brick Lane merged together under one roof.

Chungking Mansions is famous and infamous in equal measure. For those with a delicate cultural constitution it is the bête noir of Hong Kong civility, where drugs and prostitution are somehow 'legitimised' and where the worst kinds of people live. Foreigners, in other words; Hong Kong is quite an intolerant place, with one recent survey showing that seven out of ten Hong Kongers wouldn't like to live next door to someone of a different race, the highest percentage in the world. It is also a place that has had its fair share of deaths, many on account of its fire exits being bricked up. In 1988 for instance, a Danish tourist was caught in a fire on the eleventh floor, and in a fit of desperation launched himself out of the window, taking a mattress with him for a soft landing. Needless to say his plan didn't work too well.

Yet for many people, Chungking Mansions is a wonderful part of the territory's heritage, especially if you happen to be a fan of some of Hong Kong's best-known curry houses; many a sports team has ended its season with a meal at one of the renowned restaurants, such as the schoolboy smirk-worthy 'Gaylord's.' Even for those not interested in eating there—perhaps those just looking for a different experience in Hong Kong—there were plenty of fans of the old place.

It wasn't always thus. Apparently it was quite a high-end tower when it was built in 1961, even home to a couple of British Army officers. The arrival of large numbers of American servicemen during the Vietnam War turned both Wanchai and Chungking Mansions into areas of ill repute. Yet Chungking was quick to diversify away from licentiousness and into a leader of low-value international trade, a position it holds to this day. Professor Gordon Mathews, a Hong Kong anthropologist who has spent many a year studying the place, has estimated that over twenty percent of all phones in Sub-Saharan Africa pass though the building. Not all trade is legal though. Chungking was for some years a centre of the Nepali 'gold run', an eye-watering way to earn a crust if ever there was one. It being illegal to own gold in Nepal, at least in the 1980s when the practice was at its peak, travellers staying in one of the countless guesthouses would be paid to smuggle gold into the Himalayan nation inserted in their rectum. It's said that the Nepali police would strip suspects, then make them do star jumps and squats to see if anything golden came out. I'm guessing the rookie police were given that particular task, particularly if the evidence needed to be collected.

A brief pootle through the stalls and shops was all that was needed to inhale the flavours of the place. After treating ourselves to a couple of samosas—excellent, by the way—we headed onwards to our next stop of the day, which coincidentally enough was the closest thing to a Chungking Mansions of old: the Walled City of Kowloon.

Not all the soldiers in Hong Kong during British rule owed their allegiance to the British Monarch. A little-known fact is that part of the New Territories, which was ceded to the UK in 1898, remained legally part of the then Qing Empire in the form of a six acre Imperial fortress, manned for many years by the Emperor's own soldiers. The fort slowly changed to a civilian outpost as China descended into civil war, and by 1987 the area housed over thirty-three thousand people. By then the Kowloon Walled City, as it had become known, was a hotbed of both vice and manufacturing—a distinct combination it has to be said, and one well worth a peek.

We wandered towards this former Chinese outpost through the crowds of Kowloon, past cheap clothes shops and in the constant glow of twenty-four hour neon, avoiding the temptation of the copy watches and suits that were constantly offered by scrawny men in moustaches and, more often than not, white vest-tops. Persistence was their thing; even if I had been wearing a Savile Row suit and fourteen real Rolexes I'm sure they'd have still tapped me up.

After an exhaustive time on our feet, which at least allowed Larry a nice sleep in his pushchair, we arrived at the Walled City. I was not quite sure what to expect given that the place had been demolished twenty years before, but it turned out to be a splendid mix of museum and park that was worth a good few hours of strolling and reading. At one side of the site lay a metal model of what the City used to look like, and even at this small scale it was enough to give a health and safety inspector a panic attack.

Crammed in to its six acres were dozens of tower blocks, all built so that they leaned on each other but none having any foundations. According to the excellent video history of the city we watched, residents "lived day-to-day not knowing if the building would collapse or not", especially, I imagine, in typhoon season.

Each year, several of these Asian hurricanes arrived and left a trail of destruction, although, as neighbour Vivian said, at a scale much reduced compared to the past.

"Oh my God," she explained in her semi-Brooklyn drawl, "one year parts of the island were cut off for days because all the trees there were blown down. And many of the little sampans were sunk, and all the families living on them drowned, may the Lord bless their souls."

Typhoons were normally rated on a one to ten scale; anything above level eight required the whole territory to shut itself down—schools and businesses were closed, the streets emptied, and everyone returned home. This was a very wise tradition given that when the winds came they did it in style. On our first typhoon, shortly after we had moved into the Midlevels, we lay there watching the windows bulge in and out and water stream through a crack in the window frame. Dusk had come early, forced by the sheer weight of weather which then morphed into a thick, treacly black that made the night seem very close indeed. It was a distinctly unnerving experience, and I could only imagine that going through that when living in a foundationless tower would have been bloody terrifying.

Fire—so often a mass killer in Hong Kong's history—was a constant worry in the Walled City. The risk was heightened by the limitless industry that churned out products throughout the city, from fish balls to machine tools. How they managed to live and manufacture was a mystery when one considered that there were no official utilities. Water was taken from underground wells that were highly polluted by industrial effluent, forcing the population to go out into the street and into Hong Kong proper to fill up jerry cans. They then had to lug these up the stairs of their twelve-storey buildings by hand, there being only three lifts in the whole complex. To save on going down to the bottom and walking back up every time they wanted to visit a neighbouring tower block, numerous passageways were knocked through between them. As the video history showed, apart from encouraging the kids to roam, this also had the un-fortunate side effect of making it much easier for criminals and drug ad-dicts to move around.

"By day the children skipped and played on the rooftops. By night the druggies took their place, hunched in corners, their glowing pipes looking like fiery glow-worms," said an old woman who grew up there.

To add to it all, the triads controlled the place. As gambling was out-lawed in Hong Kong until 1977, the Walled City was where the locals came to bet. Old King Cnut would have had an easier time keeping the sea at bay than stopping the Chinese from gambling. The Walled City's bookmakers made a vast profit, all siphoned in one form or another to the triad gangs. This organised criminal control was part of the reason that the enclave was so hard to get rid of. The Hong Kong Government spent decades trying to demolish it, but to no avail. Local resistance—inflamed by the triads who would obviously have had much to lose—and staunch opposition from Beijing, which jealously guarded its sover-eignty of this corner of the colony, meant that several regeneration schemes were thwarted. In fact, it was only the 1984 Sino-British declara-tion that handed back Hong Kong to China, plus the legalisation of gambling seven years previously, which smoothed the way for removing the den of squalor.

We were all beginning to feel a little hot and bothered by this stage of the day, but in all honesty, we were just being thoroughly un-acclimatised. It was actually, by southern China standards, much cooler than it had been a few weeks before, a not surprising phenomena considering that it was now October. The locals were obviously feeling the chill as many of them had taken to sporting jeans and jumpers, although us Northern Europeans were still more comfortable in beach wear.

It was the concierge of our block who was the first to break the summer clothing trend, a few days before our Kowloon adventure. Sister Yi, as everyone knew her—all the female staff were called 'sister' for a reason that was never really explained to me—was neat, with a round, chubby face, and eyes that, no matter how much she smiled, always seemed a little sad. I had developed the habit of going downstairs before breakfast to pick up a copy of the China Daily newspaper, and had grown used to her wearing a short-sleeved white shirt with 'Security' boldly emblazoned across it. This particular morning she had put on a black jumper too.

"Jou-sahn!" I exclaimed. I was beginning to pick up a little of the local lingo above and beyond directing the minibuses when to stop. 'Jou-sahn' was the word for 'good morning', and I used it with gusto until midday, when 'nei-hou'—a more general 'hello'—took effect. 'Good evening' was 'Jou-tao', although as this could, iif not pronounced correctly, mean 'Fuck off', my use of it had so far had a mixed impact.

"Are you ill?" I enquired, spying her knitwear. She looked at me icily.

"No, is autumn time now. Cold coming."

"Really?" I asked, not sure if she was pulling my leg as it was twenty-nine degrees outside. But there was no doubt that she felt she needed the extra protection of the sweater. As if to prove her point, she pressed into my hand a leaflet that proclaimed that the estate's swimming pool was now 'closed for winter.' The water was still warm enough for even the most squeamish of British skinny-dippers but not, apparently, for Hong Kong levels of comfort.

This 'cold weather' was news to us. I had been in Hong Kong for December and January on my first trip, but didn't remember the weather being anything other than sunny and warm. Perhaps it was a different climate then, or maybe my memory was playing tricks. Whatever the reason, neither of us had remembered to pack anything more than the most rudimentary of winter clothing. Rather than stick out in our summer attire, it was time for us to hit the shops.

TWELVE

....

I n 2011 an American expat working in Yunnan Province, on China's southern borders, went shopping. At first, the Apple shop she visited looked legitimate, with the shelves stocked with iPads and iPods and all that would be expected; the exception was that they had managed to spell 'Apple stoer' wrong. Her curiosity piqued, she checked Apple's website and confirmed that Apple only had four official stores in China, and none were in Yunnan. Everything in the shop—the grey slate floors, steel staircases, wood benches, and staff in branded blue t-shirts, even maybe the merchandise—was fake. The expat struck up a conversation with the salespeople who, it turned out, all genuinely believed that they were working for Apple.

"I tried to imagine the training that they went to when they were hired," the expat wrote on her blog, birdabroad, "in which they were pitched some big speech about how they were working for this innovative, global company—when really they're just filling the pockets of some shyster living in a prefab mansion outside the city by standing around a fake store disinterestedly selling what may or may not be actual Apple products that fell off the back of a truck somewhere."

Unfortunately China has picked up an unsurpassed reputation for counterfeiting, as anyone that has been to Beijing's Silk Market—or indeed, been offered 'genuine DVDs' by an anorak-wearing Chinese bloke bearing a fat CD case and a shifty gaze—can attest to. Spotting counterfeits on the backstreets of Hong Kong was a great way to pep up the chore of shopping, although the sport wasn't as fun as on the Mainland, where you could buy a coffee at Sffcccks Coffee (aka Starbucks anywhere else), a bogus sabre-tooth tiger head made from a dog skull, or even fake eggs made from a concoction of chemicals so realistic that numerous upmarket restaurants had been caught adding them to dishes without any customers noticing a thing.

It was still, however, a bit of a shock to find that even one of Hong Kong's largest and best-known department stores was also getting in on the act. There, positioned right next to real Nike clothes, was a range of 'Ike' sportswear, complete with recognisable swish logo. I looked but there was, alas, no 'Weebok' or 'Daddydas'. It all looked absolutely convincing, and conceivably there could have been a legitimate Chinese brand called Ike that had no web presence, no marketing strategy, nor any existence other than in car boots and street vendors—or well-known department stores for that matter. Or alternatively it could have been a botched job by non-English speaking workers. I thought I had stumbled across another humdinger when I discovered 'Leaveland' clothing with a logo reminiscent of Timberland, but some web searches illuminated me to their provenance: Philippines, and apparently above-board. It was a good riff on the name though.

We discovered all this when out shopping for our autumnal wardrobe. The streets were filling up with autumn jackets and woollens of every kind, and the shops were booming as a result. In our personal search for a seasonable collection we had an almost unlimited supply of shops to choose from. Kowloon, or actually Hong Kong in general, could really be any affluent city in the West in terms of its shops. Actually in many ways it is more western than many western cities, with newer infrastructure and a more intense materialism. Every single notable high-end brand is here, and in massive numbers too; at the time of our arrival there were seventeen Burberry stores, ten Chanel outlets, and seven for Louis Vuitton. Each luxury store was full, all the time. It was not unknown for the staff of especially busy shops to walk up and down the ubiquitous queue outside and ask how much the shopper was planning to spend; those not reaching a certain threshold were asked to leave the line.

There was, however, an almost total lack of the middle high street; Uniqlo, Zara, and H&M had a smattering of stores combined, and Harvey Nichols possessed the same number of Hong Kong Island outlets as Gap.

Expensive brands that had almost failed back home were booming here or across in Mainland China. Kent and Curwen, founded in England in 1926 and once outfitters to the English cricket team, had all but shut up shop in their native land, with one solitary store in Bond Street. In Hong Kong there were eight K&C stores, with two more over in Macao, and an astonishing one hundred and six in the rest of China. This was a company that knew where its customers were.

Buyers of designer clothing were all aiming for the same achievement: attracting attention. No one could have accused the average Hong Konger of poor taste—there were no Russian-style silver jackets with foot-high shoulder pads on display—but people did like to look both good and expensive. This didn't mean the clothes had to be real.

Unfortunately fake clothing was not the only crime that stalked the streets. In the midst of some of Kowloon's poshest stores was a reminder that not all that happens here was wholesome. Although Hong Kong was much safer than most other territories, there was the occasional incident that made even the most seasoned crime hack choke on his cornflakes and dab an anxious brow. The Hello Kitty murder was one such event.

It's probably safe to say that the most interesting thing that happened in the Kowloon police station in 1999 was the arrival of a fourteen-year-old girl who claimed, in true horror movie style, to be haunted by the ghost of a woman that she had helped pound, murder, and cut up. Quite understandably it took the police a while to believe her, until, that is, they visited the flat where it was all meant to have happened and discovered a woman's skull rammed inside the head of a giant Hello Kitty mermaid doll.

The victim, a twenty-three-year-old prostitute called Ah Map, had made the literally fatal mistake of stealing the wallet of one of her clients, a triad gangster called Chan. As might be imagined, triads aren't the nicest of people. Although they are rumoured by some to have been founded by those Hollywood-friendly Shaolin monks, they have gained a reputation over the years as being, well, a little violent. Anyone that had seen the archetypal Hong Kong film Infernal Affairs or its American remake, The Departed would understand that you don't mess with them. This was a message firmly implanted in my mind on my first visit to the territory, when I read a story of an unfortunate triad victim who had had his lower arms and legs chopped off with meat cleavers, and was then left to bleed to death in a car park.

It was said that the triad hotspot of Hong Kong was a part of Kowloon called Mong Kok. Although the police I met denied it, I heard from old China hands that the gangsters controlled the area without much fear from official raids. The deal, as it was rumoured, was that as long as they kept things low-key they would be left alone. The case of Ah Map was when things went too far.

All in all, it was probably unwise of Ah Map to have crossed Triad Chan, as not only was he a bloodthirsty gangster, but he was also a crystal meth addict. The effect that this particular drug has on its addicts is the pharmacological equivalent to being in the SS; it makes you do crazy, evil things with terrible consequences and a vast amount of collateral damage, but you just don't care. If you want a little illuminating anecdote on what it can do, then look no further than Sydneysider Brendon McMahon. Once a successful financier, he developed a regular meth habit and was soon being prosecuted for having sexual relations with one rabbit and the sadistic killing of seventeen others. This is a drug that really melts your mind.

Poor Ah Map tried to pay the money back, plus interest, but this wasn't enough, and so she was kidnapped and taken back to Chan's place. His whole life was a drug-induced fantasy, with Hello Kitty dolls littered around his flat and computer games taking up the most part of his day—when he wasn't loan sharking, pimping, or attacking his rivals, that is.

With Chan's mind dangerously altered, Ah Map's detention was never going to be fun. She was beaten, burnt, and made to swallow urine. Helping in all this was the fourteen-year-old girl, who defecated in a box and made Ah Map eat it. At night the victim was strung up with electrical wire, hung from a ceiling hook, and beaten over and over.

"But only if there was nothing on TV," the defendants pointed out in their defence.

Eventually Ah Map gave up, much to the disappointment of her captors.

"She was broken and playing with her wasn't so much fun after that," said her young female torturer, "but we carried on anyway. There wasn't anything else to do."

Soon she was dead. Not knowing what to do with her, Chan and his accomplices went to the arcade to play more games, leaving the corpse on the apartment floor. When they returned he had a plan; they dismembered her with a wood saw, Chan personally cutting off her head. They stored her body parts in the fridge and threw some out, but they decided to boil her head to strip its flesh off. In a moment of diabolical inspiration they then sewed the skull into the Hello Kitty doll and stashed it in a cupboard. And there the remains of Ah Map lay until her fourteen-year-old assailant started seeing her ghost.

Since this horrific event it had been a touch difficult to find a buyer for the apartment where this all took place, despite its location in central Kowloon where flats would normally sell for millions. Buyers were put off not only by the infamy of the property but also by the persistent rumours of CCTV cameras in neighbourhood stores capturing a female form lingering in shops well after closing hours.

Any property with a history of unnatural death is called a 'Hongza'—a term derived from the Cantonese word 'hong', meaning violence, murder or calamity, and 'za' meaning residence. They typically sell for between ten to forty percent below market value, which makes a real difference in a city where house prices near doubled in the six years after 2006. There are of course plenty of property speculators who realise that there is a bargain to be had if the right buyer can be found. Generally these are foreigners, although whether this is because they aren't as superstitious as the locals or because the estate agent doesn't tell them about the flat's past is debatable.

One agent I noticed is happy to publicize where things have gone wrong at home, with a whole page dedicated to haunted houses. The list of properties reads like a list of Hong Kong's hidden tragedies. '106-year-old female jumps from building'; 'Indonesia man was chained with dog collar and murdered by his girlfriend'; '34 years female killed herself with burning charcoal.' Hardly a single one was reported in the press; like Asian Eleanor Rigbys, many weren't noted by anyone, apart of course from the police or the ambulance drivers.

With all this unseen death and tragedy there was a great deal that resonated with Hong Kongers at Halloween. The main difference between Hong Kong Halloween and most of the rest of the world was how many adults celebrated it. Sure children went from house to house asking for candy—'or else'—but it was harmless as the vast majority wouldn't know how to pull an evil trick if paid. By comparison, in Leicester, kids used to egg houses, sometimes using bricks, and not just at Halloween either.

Adults here really indulged in the whole dressing-up thing. On Halloween night I eschewed Tom's invitation to go to an all-night party to have a quiet drink with the wife, watching Lan Kwai Fong fill up with the most eye-catching of costumes. Given that we weren't particularly in the mood for dressing up, we sat supping our drinks surrounded by a menagerie of the scariest kind. Bleeding clowns were ten a dozen; vampiric forms thronged the streets; even the Honey Monster made an inexplicable appearance. Many Chinese youngsters had armed themselves with cameras, and surged through the crowds looking for particularly interesting people to photograph. One poor Brit had done such a good job of painting himself as a zombie that he spent twenty minutes having his picture taken, when quite obviously all he wanted to do was to drink the pint that lay agonizingly just out of reach.

With a deep interest in the spirits and the supernatural, it was only to be expected that the papers took the opportunity of Halloween to publish lists of the 'most haunted houses in Hong Kong'. These lists were not overly expansive, and always included the Hello Kitty flat, but there were some other nuggets too. One of the most heartfelt were the accounts of ashen-faced children that were often seen waving to passers-by near the New Territories town of Tai Po, a paranormal reminder of an innocent school picnic that turned to tragedy when all twenty-eight children and teachers were buried alive in a landslide.

Sadly for Hong Kong, the reason for there being numerous ghost stories was that there have been so many horrible deaths in its short history. Whether killed by a landslide, burnt to death in one of the sweeping fires that regularly gutted vast swathes of houses, or taken by the plague that kept visiting until public hygiene was properly sorted, there were a substantial number of unfortunate souls that didn't reach old age.

Yet the worst calamity to strike Hong Kong was purely man-made: the Japanese occupation of World War Two. Such was its brutality that it was no surprise so many ghost stories emanated from that time.

THIRTEEN

....

November was not beach time in Hong Kong, as most locals
thought that temperatures in their mid- to late-twenties were
far too cold to sunbathe. We on the other hand basked in
temperatures that were equal to a warm summer's day back in England,
and were excited about heading to the seashore. Sister Yi, thickly clad in
her autumnal jumper, looked rather askance as we told her our day's
plan.

The village of Shek O was possibly the most beautiful part of the island. Hong Kong's international role as a major port didn't leave it with
the cleanest shoreline—some of the beaches were dirtier than a third
world rubbish dump—but this isolated hamlet in the far south-east was
as close to spotless as we could find. It was naturally a renowned beach
destination, with plenty of restaurants and small shacks selling seaside tat
aplenty, and in good weather had visitors streaming in from all parts. We
spent the day surrounded by expats, eating ice creams under a purple
parasol, and watching a stream of Evangelical Chinese being baptized in
the shallows.

One thing I noted was just how fit and healthy all our fellow beach
bums looked. It wasn't like Blackpool beach, where there was more than
enough fat on show, but was instead much more akin to something off
Baywatch. Although I had started playing weekly hockey, paradoxically
with the Football Club, there was obviously still much more to be done

to reach the levels of tone that was exhibited all around us. It was time to get fit, but first I had a lunch to attend.

Just before we had boarded the plane to Hong Kong I had been asked to a cricket match by an old friend who wanted to introduce me to someone that he thought would be a good influence on our new life out East. Relatively tall, with a rakish white beard and a bearing that managed to be both formal and jovial at the same time, Witto was my introduction to Hong Kong high-life.

"Don't worry about a thing, old boy," he reassured me after a couple of glasses of wine together watching the English bowlers swept out of the ground, "you'll find Hong Kong very much to your liking, I assure you."

He took me under his wing with style. Within a few weeks of arriving he had invited me to dinner to meet some people that might be able to help with finding suitable employment. While none of them could or would offer me something directly, they all promised to let me know if they heard of any openings and, more importantly, each proffered their use as a sounding board if I needed to discuss any particular opportunity. For a town built on networking, these were kind and potentially very useful offers.

Another favour Witto performed was to introduce me to the Second Friday Lunch Club. This society was originally set up as a way for British military officers to meet civilians, and have good alcoholic fun in the process. That the Army set up a drinking club was hardly a surprise, given that the institution was linked to booze right from Hong Kong's beginning. In fact, the foundation of the colony seemed to coincide with a period in time that was remarkable for the amount of booze consumed. In 1835, for example, the six hundred and seventy-four men and officers of the 49th (Hertfordshire) Regiment, stationed in nearby India, managed to gorge their way through seven thousand, two hundred and sixteen gallons of arak, a local rice brandy, one hundred and seventy-seven gallons of brandy proper, and one hundred and forty-four of gin. This equates to almost ninety pints of hard liquor per man per year—and these numbers don't even include the beer and wine that they steamed through. Not surprisingly at least eighteen of them died of alcoholism. If the disease didn't kill you, then the cure quite possibly would. A few years after this Atlas-like effort by the 49th, a British officer admitted to hospital in Calcutta suffering from the DTs died after being administered successive prescriptions of brandy, camphor, tartar emetic, opium, and for some unknown reason, an enema. It was a wonder they were able to load their guns.

The Second Friday was not quite in the same drinking league, but was immensely fun nonetheless, and full of people of a wide variety of backgrounds. Interestingly there were more American servicemen at the raucous lunch I attended than their British equivalents. This was because the US consulate here continued to house American military personnel, whereas the UK obviously didn't think there was anything of military value to keep an eye on. The world's largest army and a fast developing navy and air force just across the border obviously didn't count as interesting in London's eyes.

Before handover the military had had an important role in Hong Kong. In terms of decision making, the Governor was Commander in Chief of all British forces there, and the Commander British Forces— normally a general of some kind—was an ex-officio member of the Legislative Council until 1966. There were army and navy bases scattered across the colony, and even the airport was shared with the Royal Air Force. Officers and men contributed a great deal to local life: the officers in their clubs; the ratings, soldiers, and airmen by keeping the bars, prostitutes, and police busy. Sports were heavily influenced by serving and ex-servicemen, such as the Khalsa hockey team, which, I was told, was founded by British Army Sikhs and went on to become one of the premier hockey clubs in Hong Kong.

Some might think that the British military story ended in 1997, when the People's Liberation Army swept across the border, standing erect on their green lorries and worrying the hell out of the local population. Yet the vestiges of Britain's military presence were still here if one looked hard enough.

After a chance encounter with a former British Territorial Army officer in a pub, I was asked along to the Hong Kong Ex-Serviceman's Association for drinks. Set in a warehouse in deepest Kowloon, the Association's clubhouse was the closest thing to an old British NAAFI remaining in Hong Kong. For those of you not so well acquainted with the drinking intricacies of the British squaddie, a NAAFI is where the soldiers go to eat and make merry. This place was no exception. The walls were festooned with the photos and plaques of regiments and ships that served in Hong Kong, many now long disbanded or scrapped. A bar, served by an elderly Chinese woman, was free-flowing and all you could drink for $30 (about £2.50). A buffet of tasty local food was spread opposite. With my own army background I felt immediately at home, even with the Cantonese chat and 'chink, chink' of mahjong.

I began talking to Albert Lam, MBE, the Chairman of the Association and a man whose upright disposition and kindly attitude would make him welcome in any mess. They had, he said, approximately one thousand, three hundred members, all veterans of the officiously-named Locally Employed Personnel (LEPs) that the British Armed Forces employed during the colonial years. With eighty percent of them Army—the rest being Royal Navy, as the Chinese were not allowed to join the Royal Air Force for some unknown reason—there was a distinct soldierly bent to the Association, and indeed twenty-five members still served in the Army or the UK Ministry of Defence Police. One was even serving in Afghanistan.

As you could tell from the moustache, Henry Lam was a Chinese sergeant major in the Royal Military Police. The average sergeant major has more tales than could be counted on the fingers of a regiment, and Henry was no exception. The anecdotes tended to revolve around the amazing and enduring ability of the British soldier to fight his way around the bars of the world. Did he mind having to break up yet another battle, whether it be with visiting American sailors, local Chinese, or just another regiment? No, not at all, they were nice boys on the whole, he smiled. He was not alone in having fond memories of the UK and its armed forces: "I wish I was still in" was the most common phrase of the night.

It turned out Henry didn't live in Hong Kong anymore. He moved abroad after he retired, looking for work because—according to what I heard from the ex-servicemen—they received no British Government pension. For many of the retired personnel in their forties or fifties this was a pain, but not insurmountable. For many of the men in their seventies and eighties this was a very significant blow to their lives. 'Ginger' and 'Bob' were two such octogenarians. Both white-British, they were among a number of expat ex-servicemen who still lived in Hong Kong, having married local women when stationed here. Both still had the squaddie glint in their eye. But life was not easy, explained Bob, leaning on his stick and breathing quite shallowly. The champagne and club lifestyle of the modern Hong Kong was far beyond them; they lived a much more local life.

"Which is why," Bob continued, "the Ex-Serviceman's Association is so important to us. It's a link to the past, and a place to meet friends and do what soldiers do best and talk about the old days." It was not as if you could forget them there in the clubhouse, with the memorabilia such as it is. They even had a local bagpiper play, which had everyone stamping, clapping, and cheering along to Highland Cathedral and other such tunes.

Shortly after this heady evening was Remembrance Sunday. Although it perhaps didn't mean as much to the general population as it did in Britain, Canada, and so on, it was still an important date in the calendar. Tom and I did some poppy selling on the preceding Saturday morning, perched at a gap on the Midlevels escalator, and through no special talent of ours managed to raise about $3,000 (around £250) in three hours. At least three-quarters of the contributors came from the Chinese. The remainder was mainly from the British, but Americans, Canadians, Aussies, Kiwis, and Indians all gave; the noticeable exception were the dozens of French that passed us by. Not a single Gallic penny went into the pot.

The reason why Remembrance Sunday continued to be an important day was because of what Hong Kong went through during the World Wars. As we strolled from our house to the Cenotaph, an exact replica of London's and the location of the annual multi-faith Remembrance service, we passed through the Hong Kong Botanic Gardens. The cool shade of the trees and the snuffles and cheeps from the caged wildlife made it a calm, peaceful walk. There was, however, a reminder on the path of the horrors that once came to this small part of China. A huge paifang-shaped arch sat astride the southern entrance to the park, dedicated to the Chinese who died assisting the Allies during the two World Wars. The inscription on the lintel read: "In Memory of the Chinese who died loyal to the Allied cause in the Wars of 1914–1918 and 1939–1945."

The local population, both white and Chinese, made a significant effort to the First World War, with many locals serving aboard Royal Navy and Merchant Navy vessels. Five hundred and seventy-nine out of a total of two thousand, one hundred and fifty-seven mainly British volunteers opted for military service outside the colony. In addition, aside from the normal financial contribution made to the war effort by the Empire's constituent parts, Hong Kong paid a further $10 million, equivalent to total government revenue for 1914. Individual Chinese made significant contributions too, such as fighter aircrafts, which at least one local historian believed to have been a "reflection of the appreciation the better-off Chinese had for the British administration."

Come WWII and it was a very different story. Hong Kong itself was invaded, a mere eight hours after Pearl Harbor.

The garrison here had no chance. The Japanese, with fifty-two thousand battle-hardened troops, outnumbered the fourteen thousand British, Canadians and Indians—backed up by the Hong Kong Volunteer Defence Force—four to one. The vast majority of the defenders had no field experience; most of the Canadians had only been in the colony for three weeks following an arduous posting to the bars and beaches of Jamaica, and there was no air or naval cover. Add to this the fact that most of the heavy equipment being shipped over for the defence of Hong Kong had been diverted to other territories, and the defenders were in a tight spot.

The fact that the odds were so utterly stacked against them didn't seem to overly affect the defenders. In fact, some took the opportunity to rise to the occasion. Captain Mateen Ahmed Ansari was one of these. An Indian aristocrat, he arrived in Hong Kong as both a junior lieutenant in the 7th Rajputs and, rather inharmoniously, as a determined Indian nationalist. Balancing the incompatibility was by all accounts a difficult task, and he was renowned for having a number of highly undesirable friends in the colony. But come the Japanese and a remarkable transformation took place. After a distinguished defensive campaign—war seemed to have brought out some remarkable qualities in him as a leader and a soldier—he was eventually captured, and given his social position and views on India was initially well treated by the Japanese. However, his old nationalistic ways had been somewhat diminished by the fighting, and he thus refused to help subvert his fellow Indian prisoners of war to join the Japanese cause. The result was that he was thrown into prison. Starved and tortured, he was eventually beheaded alongside thirty other prisoners. Not many other Indian nationalists were awarded a posthumous George Cross for conspicuous gallantry.

Many of the defenders were in reality civilians. Major Henry Forsyth, an expatriate Scot who worked for HSBC, was typical of those who had joined the Hong Kong Volunteers. A veteran of WWI, he had come out to Asia to escape from the post-war depression of a grey Europe, only to find himself once again surrounded by war. He and his best friend from the bank, a man named Swan, found themselves towards the end of the battle defending the approach to the south-coast town of Stanley, manning a machine gun to keep the Japanese at bay. As the war diary for the day notes, "Major Forsyth is again wounded seriously and Company Sergeant-Major T. Swan is killed, and Forsyth is carried to the schoolhouse adjoining Stanley old police station." This was in the midst of some of the heaviest fighting of the entire campaign.

"Nearby, on our left," wrote one Gunner Bertram of the 2 Battery, Hong Kong Volunteer Force, "a house was surrounded, Bren guns blazing from each quarter and automatics returning the fire at point-blank range. All over the place were similar close exchanges. I had never guessed that a real battle could be so like a gangster film." What makes it all the more poignant is that there was almost zero chance of anyone coming to relieve the defenders.

The battle raged for eighteen days, the same length of time that Belgium held out against the Germans, until final surrender occurred on Christmas Day 1941. Interestingly the final fighting was not wrapped up until two days after the official cease-fire, taking place in an ammo bunker at the centre of the island, which was now—surely to the delight of old soldiers everywhere—a wine-drinking den. According to local legend, the defenders of the bunker so impressed the Japanese with their bravery that they were let go after the battle rather than be interned.

Both the British and Japanese had each lost around two thousand men. Many of the defenders were slaughtered after surrendering, including the military hospital at Stanley where around one hundred and seventy patients and staff were tortured to death, with their ears, noses, and other protuberances cut off; the nurses raped and killed; and the young orderlies, many of them boys of only fifteen, sixteen, or seventeen, herded together and then bayoneted or pushed off a cliff.

The local Chinese really suffered too, in fact much more than the Westerners, with four thousand of them dying during the battle alone. But worse was to come. Four brutal years of Japanese occupation followed, which saw the population of Hong Kong drop from one point six million to six hundred thousand as a consequence of forced repatriation and murder. A favourite method of impromptu execution, metered out to random locals for nothing more than being in the wrong place at the wrong time, was to force a hose down the victim's throat and pump in water until the stomach burst. An estimated ten thousand Chinese women were raped by the invader garrison, many of them decapitated and dumped in the street for their families to find. It's no surprise that the Japanese Governor, an owlish general called Hisakazu Tanaka who looked more like a bicycle salesman than a war criminal, was executed after the war. It was a fitting end to the most sadistic, brutal time in Hong Kong's history.

FOURTEEN

....

O n one Friday evening we went out with some new friends, a South African couple that had, coincidentally enough, arrived the exact same day we had. Yet, whereas Aggie had had a few days to settle down, poor Cameron had been forced to abandon Chlöe to the unpacking by starting work less than three hours after his plane had touched down. Such was the way of some employers.

It was good to be going out with newly arrived friends, because we were beginning to notice something of Hong Kong social life that we hadn't really expected. Tom and I had discussed the fact that the majority of people we saw on a (semi-) regular basis were generally those that had pitched up at a similar time to us. This, I suppose, is natural, as you can often have more in common with someone in the same situation as you than someone who is a few years ahead in the Hong Kong lifestyle.

Another important element in friend-making was avoiding those who weren't going to be around for at least a couple of years.

"Have you noticed that the first question anyone seems to ask when they meet you is 'How long are you in Hong Kong for?'?" I had indeed, as we had been subject to that interrogative many times already.

"It's because if you say less than two years then they don't want to waste time making friends with you." This also made sense I suppose, but as we didn't yet know how long we would stay, it was a little concerning that our social life was being partly designed by how many years we would stick around for. Not surprisingly, from that moment on we always described ourselves as being in Hong Kong 'indefinitely'.

Obviously I already had Tom as a good pal, but we both needed new friends, and ones that enjoyed other pursuits apart from drinking and growing a beer belly.

Cameron and Chlöe were the perfect foil for Tom's partying. Thoroughly laid-back and passionate about walking and the outdoors in general, they had the added attraction of introducing us to Reuben. He was a friendly, young American guy with thick eyebrows that resembled an over-watered bramble, and a disarming smile that made him someone to instantly take to. We knew we were going to like Reuben as soon as we went to the bar. I ordered a round of beers for everyone, but Reuben declined. Instead he ordered his own beer, with a couple of vodka chasers.

"Want some shots?" he asked us.

"Um, it's 6.15—maybe a bit later."

"OK, but just shout when you want some." And with that he ordered two more.

Reuben's drinking prowess was matched only by his geographical ineptness. As we all chatted about South Africa, I noticed he kept looking at his iPhone.

"So where's Cape Town?" he asked after a story from Cameron's youth. Perhaps this was a fair question to those that hadn't visited the country. But every time another city, in any country, was mentioned, out came the phone. It turned out he had never been out of state before he arrived in Hong Kong, and that state was Pennsylvania, hardly one of America's largest. But he had seen the job advert for a role out East, had applied, and suddenly here he was. That's brave; to have never even been to New York and yet decide you're moving to the other side of the world to somewhere that is, outside of the few streets of Soho and Central, really quite foreign.

Reuben's past seemed like a long time ago when we woke up the next morning, late and in pain. I had a vague memory that we had all agreed to do some joint exploring, and soon a text message from Cameron confirmed as much. Not many minutes later and we were on a ferry to the island of Cheung Chau.

Although its name in Cantonese meant Long Isle, it had over the last decade developed a new moniker: Suicide Island. For some reason, which no one really understood, the turn of the millennium saw the dawn of a spate of people killing themselves on Cheung Chau. The majority were visitors to the island, and they mainly ended it all by sealing themselves in their holiday cottages, setting fire to some charcoal, and passing away thanks to the resulting carbon monoxide. Quite why the use of charcoal became the method of choice is also something of a mystery, although possibly it was because of the myth that it was 'easy and painless' compared to other options, despite the fact that it was known to give its victims a cracking headache and the very real possibility of permanent brain damage rather than death. But death by charcoal had become a not insignificant phenomenon, on Cheung Chau in particular. One hundred and nineteen poor souls tried to end it all there between 1998 and 2004 alone, with sixty-three of them succeeding. As could be imagined, the epidemic had generated numerous reports of ghostly and horrific apparitions, and rumours had even circulated which were reminiscent of the horror movies The Ring and The Grudge. It didn't make an overnight stay on the island too palatable.

Luckily Cheung Chau was also known for something far more jolly, namely its annual bun festival. This was a week-long party originally started as a way of giving thanks for escaping bubonic plague, which seemed to be at the root of quite a few of Hong Kong's ceremonies. There were parades and lion dances and children dressed up as mythological creatures. The highlight though had to be the bun towers—literally sixty foot towers of buns—up which young locals scrambled in a competition to collect as many lucky pastries as possible within three minutes. It was just as random as other food-based festivals across the world, like cheese rolling in England or tomato throwing in Spain, but it was far sweeter tasting.

Alas the festival was a victim of its own success, with many families put off by the sheer crush of spectators. Luckily there were plenty of other reasons to visit the island, and hiking came near the top of the list. With Larry able to ride on my back much more easily than walking, our choice of routes around Hong Kong was somewhat narrowed to those that didn't have eighty degree slopes involved, lest my knees snapped. Happily Cheung Chau was home to an almost flat, circular route that we embarked upon with our hiking pals, Cameron, Chlöe, and Reuben.

Although it was early, there were still hundreds of fellow hikers, including a woman who had come in knee-length black leather boots and a short silver skirt. It was hard to tell whether she was executing a long walk of shame or if she really thought that this was good walking gear, but whichever it was, she looked mightily uncomfortable. Soon we had taken a turning that led us away from the crowds and plunged us into thick, dark woods that absorbed our voices and seemed to be quite in keeping with the morbid feel that Cheung Chau had gradually become associated with.

"Look out!" cried Reuben. Before I could do anything he had grabbed my arm and yanked me back. He pointed upwards to where, at face height to Larry sitting high above on my shoulders, there was a huge web strung across the path. In its spiral centre was a black and gold spider as large as my hand. Poor Larry wouldn't have known what had hit him.

"I think it's only a golden orb spider," said Cameron. "They're not too poisonous," he added, not too convincingly, but enough to placate me and Aggie who were a touch, well, disturbed by the near miss. Five minutes of mobile Googling later and he was proved right, but the fact that "they eat snakes and small birds" didn't necessarily comfort us. Not surprisingly the party subsequently adopted a protective pose, with Reuben walking ahead with a stick upright to catch the webs before they did an Alien facehugger impression on junior.

The rest of the walk was thankfully uneventful, apart from stumbling across a series of wooden statues of various animals hidden amidst the trees and with no sign of ownership, or even care. Ignoring this weird interlude to the walk, we headed down to the waterfront for a lunch of Nepalese curry before taking the bumpy ferry back to Central.

All this being out and about was a potential distraction to my finding a job. Luckily enough Aggie was still going great guns at work, and had quickly adapted to the role. But nothing had emerged for me, or at least anything attractive enough to rush into. This was all pretty disappointing, and was the source of quite a few heated discussions between us. To be frank, I was enjoying my Mandarin lessons and spending time with Larry, so I wasn't in the greatest of rushes to find suitable employment. But Aggie was unimpressed with this laid-back approach to income generation, and so, in the interest of family harmony, I gave myself until Christmas to find a permanent role. As it was by now nearly the end of November I had a little less than four weeks to make this come true.

Happily enough for the extrovert, job seeking in Hong Kong was pretty reliant on networking and personal referrals. This was all made simpler by the wonderful welcome that most people showed to an enquiring phone call. At first I was a bit nervous of telephoning strangers with whom it had been recommended I talk, but with the vast majority of people I spoke to being so friendly, I was soon talking to more people than a flirtatious concierge. Some wanted to meet for a coffee, others preferred a chat on the blower, but all made it clear that making time for those new in town was the done thing in Hong Kong.

"After all," one of Witto's friends confided in me over a beer, "we've all been where you're sitting."

In addition there were also the official networking drinks, generally organised by Chambers of Commerce and renowned for being the home of the 'Hong Kong handshake'—or the exchange of business cards. As I soon found out, these little oblongs were so central to meeting people that it was sometimes possible to be talking to someone whilst a card from an unknown and even unseen hand was thrust into one's palm. Turning up to a function with no card was akin to arriving dressed in a clown's suit—people would look at you for a brief moment before writing you off as not serious. There was even a little lane in Sheung Wan, just to the west of Central, where every stall was dedicated to card production, their owners trying to outcompete on both cost and the luxuriousness of the card's texture.

Soon all this networking paid off, albeit in a temporary fashion. After discussions with a construction company, an environmental start-up, and an import/export company, none of which led to anything, I had two strokes of luck. One was an interview for a large bank which sounded interesting, even though I wasn't quite sure that my non-finance CV would be overly relevant. The other was even better, being a consultant to a small Hong Kong TV company. The former may have had longer-term prospects, but the allure of television was quite hard to resist; I had after all paid for my university beer by being a film extra (you can just about see me in the movie Eyes Wide Shut, although I always hasten to add I was fully clothed, to the audience's absolute relief).

Sadly Craig, a charismatic Tasmanian with a love of beer and travel, wasn't in a position to pay me, but it was going to be fun—and a good introduction to working out East. At least Aggie's job was still providing income so, in the absence of anything else, I decided to give it a go and hope that it would eventually lead to something paid.

Although my job hadn't quite worked out as we wanted, at least we were all still healthy. But then December happened, and Aggie developed a lung disease.

FIFTEEN

....

S tanding on a promontory at the far south of the island, Stanley was a pleasant place to escape the hubbub of the Midlevels on a weekend. Before the British came it was the site of a small village of fisher folk, and the headquarters of a famous pirate called Cheung Po Tsai. Nowadays it felt like an English seaside town, home to soulless pubs and chain restaurants like Pizza Express and full of day trippers, but with the added and unexpected role as a depository for unwanted buildings. Murray Barracks Officers' Mess, an elegant, classically styled building replete with Doric and Ionic columns that dated from 1844, was a victim of the clearing of Hong Kong's colonial heritage in the early 1980s, in the same wave of clearance that did for the Repulse Bay Hotel and many other notable colonial buildings. Happily the government decided to preserve the building when its site in Central was given to the new Bank of China Tower, so it was dismantled and resurrected at a site in Stanley. Soon it was joined by another Central landmark, Blake Pier, which now sat alongside the Murray building like a pair of old timers relaxing by the sea.

Getting to Stanley was an adventure in itself, especially if you took the bus. It was a pretty safe bet that when they designed the original double-decker they didn't have the hillside roads of Hong Kong in mind. This didn't stop the drivers from plying their trade up and down the mountains and passes of the island, at high speed and low comfort. The trip from Central to Stanley should have been a picturesque one, looping over the massif of the island via Happy Valley and the glittering Repulse and Deep Water Bays, but with the bus drivers treating the route like a warm-up for Le Mans it was often a stomach-churning ordeal. A friend made the interesting choice of taking his elderly grandmother to Stanley on said bus.

"Come and sit at the front of the top deck, Grandma, you'll get a better view," was his advice, which she foolishly followed. The bus took off at speed, and didn't slow down. Her hands were wrapped tight around the bar in front of her, eyes frozen in sheer fright as the bus listed around corners at angles it wasn't designed to take, the rock of the mountainside only inches from the window.

"Are you alright Grandma? You're awfully quiet." A noise like a mouse caught in a trap came back, followed by the sound of knuckles snapping like matchsticks. After a triple gin in Stanley and a turn on the inhaler it was decided that a taxi under the mountain might be a better way to return.

One day after lunch in early December I decided to take a break from job-searching and head to Stanley for the afternoon. Since neither of us was too bad with heights, Larry and I took the high road, arriving not in the least the worse for the experience. Now, most visitors to Stanley headed there for the market, an indoor labyrinth of stalls selling the island's largest concentration of tat, with everything from novelty projectors to humdrum children's clothes. Rather than get sucked into a maelstrom of haggling tourists we slipped past the market and headed instead a short way out of town to an old temple. It was said that this was once linked to the old pirate Cheung, but it was more notable now for a sign attached to a branch just outside the entrance warning visitors to 'mind their head', notwithstanding that it was a good fifteen foot above the ground. With no one around and the air warm and lightly blowing, we sat down on a bench and watched the small fishing craft gently bob in the bay. The trees around us were full of sparrows and wagtail-like birds, chattering and hopping between the branches, and we even spotted a bird of prey swooping down to nab a fish from the sea. It was a delightful spot.

For some reason, it appeared that Stanley's local tourist board were concerned that this picture of wildlife perfection wouldn't be enough to entice the more discerning visitor, particularly those wanting to see more insects. The answer had been to build a butterfly garden, which would have been a fantastic idea had there been any butterflies in it. It's not as if Hong Kong is lacking in these creatures, as they are everywhere and often resemble small birds in their size. There are in fact twenty-nine species of butterfly listed as being present in urban parks, so we followed the signs to the Butterfly Garden with a keen sense of anticipation, expecting at any moment to turn a corner and see a cornucopia of colour fluttering in the sea breeze.

The search went on for a long ten minutes. We saw some grass, a few trees, the back of an electricity substation, and even a cat, but no butterflies. After several sweeps of the area I thought I was going blind until I stubbed my toe on an ugly metal figure, which looked very much like a Year Ten metal working project gone wrong. It was, as the accompanying sign revealed, the actual site of the elusive Butterfly Garden, that and the small patch of dirty lawn that it sat on. I thought about registering a complaint with the tourist board for draining away minutes of my life I'd never get back, but decided a drink was a much more constructive use of my time.

We thus headed back to town, looking for somewhere to have our sea-side beer and milk. Not surprisingly Larry was soon bored and, dropping his beaker, leapt from his chair and sprinted off in the direction of the sea. I sipped my ale one last time and, sapped by the day's activities, wearily went off after him, barrelling through the throng of kids coming home from school. I had just about reached him when he tripped on the pavement, hitting the deck with some force and cutting his lip. Luckily it was only minor damage, but there was enough blood to make it look like a butcher's shop. All around me people stopped and stared at the wailing, bleeding child and his irresponsible father, tutting in unison. All I could think of though was not the disapproval of strangers, but how on earth I was going to explain this to my wife. I would have to use the journey home to come up with a really, really good excuse.

Part of the shock exhibited by the locals who saw me scooping up my bleeding child was undoubtedly because this kind of scene is highly infrequent with Chinese families, where the parents are renowned for being highly protective of their children. One mother told me that she had forbidden her son from being jiggled on his father's knee lest he fell off and hurt his head. While this was an extreme example it was not exactly common to see the local offspring roughing and tumbling as they would have done in the UK, for better or worse. A degree of this undue anxiety may have stemmed from the fact that so many families only had one child, compared to a fertility rate of almost two in Britain. This was, so I learnt from neighbour Vivian, as she dropped off a huge bag of freshly made cookies, because "most of the young couples can't afford to pay for more than one kid, and apartments here are so small that you wouldn't want a big family anyway."

One upside of not having so many children was that you didn't have to stress too much about choosing a name. It soon became apparent that Chinese names are a whole world of muddle. For a start, there aren't that many of them, which makes life quite confusing at times. There are only around a thousand surnames here, but spread amongst one point three billion people. This is the same as the population of the UK only having forty-six to choose from. Zhang, Wang, Li, Chen, and Liu are among the most popular, Zhang topping the numbers game with seventy million Chinese souls. It isn't just surnames that are an issue. As most people have first names of a familiar nature, being named after every day items like 'sun', 'star', 'wave', and so on, there is considerable scope for nominative bottlenecks here too.

Consequently, there are many, many people in China who have the same name. New Moon (Wang) pointed out the issue with this.

"Imagine if you find you cannot use your bank account and the police think you are a trouble maker because someone of the same name in a different part of China got in trouble." As a result of this, the government is trying to diversify the name base. Parents are being encouraged to choose hybrid names for their kids, combining part of a father's name with part of a mother's name to create something completely original. This may lead to a decrease in cases of identity fraud, but I read that most Chinese think these new names sound daft. Not only that, in a country where ancestor worship is central to the spiritual life of many, not naming a child after one's forebears is considered strange if not decidedly risky.

One benefit of these new names may be to reduce some of the more hurtful monikers that parents sometimes felt the need to give their offspring. It is not unheard of for example for girls to be given the name 'Inviting Brothers', which has the meaning of her being taken as a good luck token for male children to follow. As New Moon pointed out, "These girls have to go through life not with a name for themselves but as a prayer for a little boy."

It soon became apparent that Hong Kong had its fair share of utterly bonkers names. We came across folk called things that in the UK would never make it onto the birth certificate. Names such as 'Stay Awhile Li', 'Panda Wang', and our personal favourite, 'A Little Bit Lu', all stuck in the mind. These eye-catchers were partly the result of people wanting to make themselves stand out from the crowd, as many people chose a Western name when they started school; for others it was a result of bad English. For some though there was no reason. At the Football Club there was a waitress called Kevin.

I bring this up because it was the run up to Christmas, and there's nothing that strikes more fear into the heart of small people than the thought of Santa Claus confusing them with some other child. It was fair to say that the Hong Kong Chinese took their Christmases seriously, at least on the face of it. With many of them staunchly Christian, and the rest mercantile enough to know a good trading bandwagon to climb on when they saw it, the run up to the twenty-fifth of December was a thoroughly active time.

Like the UK and much of the rest of the West, Christmas festivities started early. Seasonal muzak was being piped through the shopping malls from the end of November, and adornments followed rapidly. There seemed to be an unwritten competition to host the most magnificent, as well as the most wasteful, decorations possible. We took Larry over to Kowloon to look at the Star House Christmas lights and were amazed to find a whole herd of reindeer with a fat Santa Claus by their side. Although their bodies were all quite accurate in shape and size, the facial expressions of the deer were something quite different; the sculptor had apparently captured the unique moment that, whilst lying on their death beds, they had been rudely surprised by the insertion of a large suppository. It was certainly memorable.

As big fans of Christmas we launched into the spirit of things with warm enthusiasm. We had brought with us from the UK a fair amount of our Christmas decorations, but first of all we needed a tree to put them on. Unusually the only place we could readily find to buy one was Ikea, but to bring it back home I had to give a taxi driver an extra $100 to take the tree in his car. I wasn't sure where the tree had originally come from—when I asked the Ikea assistant, he helpfully told me it was "from a field"—but it was a luscious and verdant as any back in the UK. True, a small haystack of needles was soon deposited on our sitting room floor, which Larry took great delight in attempting to eat, but it generally held up well to the stresses of a mild Hong Kong December.

Because of the comparative heat, and notwithstanding the tree and tinsel, deep down it just didn't feel as Christmassy as the plentiful decorations would have justified. As the big day approached, the temperatures did start to decrease but it still didn't help. At heart it still felt like late autumn. We did buy Larry a small puffa jacket in a nod to the falling mercury, and insisted he wear it one Saturday afternoon when we went to the Victoria Park to play on the patchy grass. Overlooked by a couple of Indonesian helpers, we watched him run around chasing a ball until he almost fainted from heat exhaustion. Lesson learnt, we retired for an ice cream and a deck chair.

SIXTEEN

....

A nother twist on our Hong Kong Christmas run-up was the office party. Raised on a diet of English affairs, which normally involve drunkenly swaying around handbags with one hand holding a chardonnay and the other vainly groping for the office hottie, we were surprised to be invited to Hong Kong's largest theme park for a family Christmas do.

Ocean Park had been closed for the day to give all Aggie's colleagues free rein to go on the Mine Train/Raging River/Space Wheel as often as possible. And enjoy it they did. Some eight thousand employees, most of them young and in the mood for a good time, raced around the park whoopin' and a-hollerin' and getting under the feet of the more elderly managers. Every so often we would bump into a senior executive, perhaps nursing a coke or a hotdog, who would invariably look slightly out of place, like a farmer at a London nightclub. This uncomfortableness was made even more intense when everyone was called together for the lucky draw. For some reason the local Chinese were obsessed with these. I had heard of other Christmas parties where the staff would turn up in time for the draw then, assuming there was no free food to keep them around any longer, would stream back to the elevators as soon as there were no more pink or blue tickets to hold up.

Gweilos don't seem to have the same intense feelings about this form of selective prize distribution, as was made clear when we were waiting for my wife's CEO, a big bear of a Chinese man wearing a natty black polo jumper underneath a smart Chesterfield overcoat. He had one job, which was to pull out the raffle tickets from the pot. Thousands of Chinese, all wrapped in thick coats as the weather was a cool twelve degrees, waited in silence for the numbers to be read out. The expats meanwhile, all located at the edges of the gathering, supped their mulled wine and chatted quietly amongst themselves.

"Blue forty-three!" announced the CEO. A simultaneous wave of anger and disappointment swept through the crowd.

"Yes, yes, yes!" A young girl leapt up and dashed forward, her thick glasses jiggling on her gleeful face as she ran. Her colleagues looked on jealously, dark eyes stabbing her at every step.

After half an hour of small prize giveaways, mainly in paper money as is the tradition here, the CEO grew bored of reading out the tickets and called upon his senior management team to take over. The look of horror on the mainly expat team was something to behold. With no volunteers, a wiry Kiwi in a dark corduroy jacket and chinos was commanded to come up to the stage, his grimace suggesting that he was not particularly excited about his forced contribution. He put a thin arm into the barrel, withdrew it slowly and, peering into the throng over his metal-framed glasses, quietly read out the details.

There was silence, for about five seconds only, but it was enough. Suddenly a huge fanfare of Cantonese erupted, then a countdown began.

"No one has that ticket! Pull out another! Pull out another!" the crowd panted. It felt like being present for a lynching.

"Er," said the Kiwi. The CEO leaned over him, said a word or two, and the corduroy arm reached into the barrel again. The replacement ticket was read out.

"It's me!" A Chinese man launched a fist into the air, and sprinted through his colleagues towards the stage.

"I won!" came another cry, a blink of an eye after the first, and a second hand was raised aloft.

With two men now surging towards him, the Kiwi's eyes widened and a look of fearful panic flashed across his cheeks. He took a couple of steps back until he hit the bulk of his unmoving CEO. Someone hadn't heard the ticket number properly; either that or one of the supposed winners was seriously testing his luck. Fortunately—or more likely through bitter experience—the party organiser was prepared. Several large looking bouncers, in black bomber jackets and sporting hair like shaved carpet, intercepted the rival claimants before they could leap onto the stage. The CEO did as his position demanded. He strode forward, dismissing the weedy Kiwi with a slight shoulder charge, and plucked out a new ticket. If you want a job doing properly, or at least audibly...

Soon it was Christmas Day. Rather than eat our turkey at home, and despite the Mandarin Oriental Hotel being able to deliver a cooked bird with all the trimmings for a not-too-exorbitant sum, we decided to head out to join other celebrants and not feel totally cut off from the outside world. So after a very English church service at the cathedral, we went up to the Peak for lunch.

Everywhere the British went in Asia they developed hill stations as a refuge from the heat of the plains. Simla in India was probably the most famous, but there were many others too. In Hong Kong wealthy Europeans started building houses on and around Victoria Peak, a mountain overlooking the harbour and also known as Mount Austin or just the Peak, to escape both the high temperatures below and the tropical diseases that tended to sweep away colonists in vast numbers. The most usual way to get up and down the mountainside was by sedan chair, which must have been really rather uncomfortable at anything above a snail's pace but was still highly popular, at least until the Peak tram was built in 1888. One of the most colourful of the colony's mid-Victorian inhabitants, the Jewish opium dealer and entrepreneur Emanuel Raphael Belilios, took Peak transport one stage further by using pack camels.

The Peak was not the most obvious place to have a comfortable home. For a start, it wasn't that comfortable. Shrouded in mist for most of the year, it meant that houses were almost permanently saturated, with "envelopes all glued together and cigars like bits of sponge" as one governor noted. The Peak was also, and continues to be, a metonymy of Hong Kong's social structure. With the Governor's hill-station residence, Mountain Lodge, at the pinnacle, surrounded by the most expensive houses, the social hierarchy descended as one stepped down the mountain. As one writer from the early 1900s put it, "The Peak looks down on everything and everyone. The lower levels look up to the Peak." If the house prices on the Peak were anything to go by, where a run-of-the-mill flat cost £200,000 a year in rent, not much had changed.

Thankfully it was possible to enjoy the views from the top without having to live there. Many visitors, especially foreign tourists, took the Peak Tram to the summit. This was one of the world's steepest railways and almost unchanged since it was built by a Swiss engineer—not surprisingly given the terrain. It was also one of the few aspects of Hong Kong to have survived the years intact. As such it was hugely popular, so we took a taxi to the top instead. Much of the Peak has been remodelled over time, and is almost completely different to the pre-war years. Then there was Mountain Lodge, the Mount Austin Barracks, and the Peak Hotel, all now lost. All that remained was the old Peak Café, a Swiss-style chalet that may have been inspired by the Swiss-made trains used on the Peak Tram. Unfortunately, the old-world charm of the café was not matched by its food. Our Christmas lunch consisted of a solitary piece of rubbery turkey, two rock-like potatoes and a half-dozen Brussels sprouts. At least the decorations were plentiful, covering every inch of the walls, although it did look like a rip-off display from Poundland. They also made the effort of providing a Santa for the kids. He may have had a strong Yorkshire accent and the manners of a drunk Russian policeman, but he gave Larry a toy, so it wasn't all bad.

As it was our first family Christmas abroad we had a lot of Skyping to do; we had actually put aside most of the afternoon and early evening to calling our dispersed family. Mindful of this, we started the long walk home still a tad peckish. Happily Larry took our mind off our partial hunger by stepping in a gigantic dog poo. Although we cleaned it up as best we could, I was not particularly willing to have him on my shoulders after that, but soon had to relent after it became apparent that a four mile walk was more than a two-year-old could manage. He was soon smearing the front of my Christmas jumper with the remains of canine crap, but at least he got a good view from his shoulder perch.

SEVENTEEN

....

O
h, I don't feel well," Aggie moaned as she rolled out of bed on Boxing Day. Pre-Larry this would have been the standard post-Christmas hangover, but she had hardly been knocking it back so perhaps it wasn't a feint. In actual fact, she hadn't been on top form for the previous week, thanks to a punishing run up to Christmas which had seen her working fifteen hour days, finalising a project that had to be done before year-end.

I suggested that, if she felt a tad under the weather, we didn't have to go on the walk we had planned around Tai Tam Tuk Reservoir.

"No, I'll be alright. The fresh air will do me good."

The British are a curious race when it comes to walking. They have turned what in most of the world is a daily chore into a pastime, and a highly popular one at that. It even has its own uniform: sturdy boots; blue cagoule; beige walking trousers with cavernous side pockets; and fleece, often a dark green or red, although some crazy cats have been seen in yellow. Oh, and some kind of hat is normally in order too. Add a plastic map case and a small pack containing crushed egg sandwiches, a water bottle and some Kendal mint cake, and the outfit is complete.

When I was young we went to the Brecon Beacons in Wales each summer for a long weekend, and on our family ambles around the old monastery we stayed in we would often see these adventurous types. They always seemed to be striding off into a low bank of cloud, or being swept along by a sturdy breeze. I never saw the fun in exposing oneself to the elements—even with a cagoule—but then I joined the British Army, and realised that marching around the countryside could actually be quite fun.

The fact is, back in Britain there was a lot to like about walking, at least recreationally. There were plenty of pretty places to visit, and the view from up high was always better than in a car. No matter how many scree slopes we scrabbled up, or knife edges we balanced along, or crags we leapt over, it was supremely satisfying to reach the top, then to sit down to quietly chew our by now completely mangled egg rolls, and share the vista with some fellow walker.

Britain was a superior place to walk for more reasons than the view; it was also supremely difficult to die doing it. Sure, there were several folks a year who fell off edges or slipped into a bog in winter and froze to death, but unless I chose to go out in a mankini in the middle of winter, then it was highly unlikely I'd cark it.

A big part of this is that there was little in the way of deadly wildlife. In some parts of the world being eaten by a bear was not uncommon—in India they even had a sloth bear that "ripped out the eyes of its victims" and ended up having to be tracked and shot. The British Isles, in contrast, lost its last ursine sometime before the Norman Conquest. In late 2012 packs of wolves with highly dubious intentions attacked the villages of Eastern Russia; there hadn't been a freshly shot wolf in Scotland since 1680. Banana sellers walking through Queen Elizabeth National Park in Uganda take it as read that a good few of them will be lion food by the end of the year. Not even David Bellamy wanted Panthera leo wandering the Sussex Downs.

Here in Hong Kong it was slightly different. While, as we shall see, tigers used to prowl these parts, there hadn't been a big cat here for many a decade. But snakes and spiders did abound, and some of them had severe anger management issues. A few years ago, it was said, a number of old people started to go missing in Lantau Island, and a rumour started that they were being picked off by local serpents—probably a Burmese python, of the sort that were running amok in the Florida Everglades much to the horror of the shrinking local wildlife. The sad fact though, at least if you were an ophiophilist or a snake yourself, was that snakes large enough to kill a man were exceedingly rare in Hong Kong these days, thanks to the many snake hunters that earned a living by catching the creatures for the Cantonese pot. Back in 1996 I had visited a snake restaurant in Guangzhou and had looked on amazed at the rabbit hutch full of vipers, cobras, constrictors—every conceivable type—ready to be chosen for the table. I watched as the waiter put his leather-gloved hand into the slithering mass and pulled out a small cobra. With his left hand he proceeded to remove its head with a pair of scissors, which plopped onto the floor and was then booted into the corner. The still-wriggling animal then had its skin removed like plastic wrapper being removed from a Peperami, before being chopped up for the frying pan. It was engaging if not a little upsetting for those not used to fresh reptile soup.

Snakes weren't just in the wild or in restaurants. There were plenty of reports of them being found in and around houses, especially in the more rural New Territories. A friend of mine, Rob, lived way up north and was thus lucky to have a small garden where his daughters could play and he and his wife could sunbathe. True, this meant he had a pretty long commute to work, but it was worth it because what he also had was a shed. There is something alluring about a shed, particularly if you are male, and especially if you like sorting through the piles of rubbish that generally end up being stored there. This was exactly what Rob was doing one morning when he noticed a quick and lively motion from the corner of his eye. He instinctively knew it was a snake, so threw a blanket over it and called out to the geriatric Chinese handyman, Jimmy, to come and give him a hand.

"What's happening Dad?" asked the youngest daughter, standing at the doorway with her sister.

"Nothing, it's just a snake. We're going to capture it and let it go in the jungle over there," replied Rob.

"You're not going to kill it?" asked Jimmy, now on the scene and looking anxious to get stuck in, despite his age. The fact he was carrying a sharpened spade and a hammer were clues to his intentions.

"Dad, you're not going to kill the snake, are you?" implored the girls, almost in tears.

"No, no, of course not. Now just stand back and watch us catch it."

But Jimmy shook his head gravely.

"We cannot catch it, it is very poisonous. It has a head like an arrow. We must destroy it." And with that he slowly reached down to pick up the blanket. The snake was coiled up and hissing, not surprisingly, but managed to put on a nifty burst of speed when Jimmy started trying to whack it with his shovel. Age had the better of him though, and all his blows were wide of the shifting target. With the snake now pretty pissed off Rob thought better of trying to corral it, and so grabbed the hammer from Jimmy and joined in the fray.

"Dad, Dad, what are you doing?" screamed the sisters.

"I'm just helping Jimmy, don't worry," he breathed, trying to take aim while the handyman continued his highly ineffective spade assault. With clanking and screaming in his ears, it was only after he managed to maim the serpent that Rob realised that the hammer was the singularly most unwise weapon to use in the circumstances. In order to hit the target he had to put his unprotected hand within a foot of the angry snake's fangs, and with the high likelihood that the beast was going to be faster than an early-middle-aged Brit suffering from a hangover, it was not going to end well for him.

Nonetheless, Rob was somehow able to land a glancing blow, which stunned the poor animal long enough for Jimmy to cut its head off. It took about three days for his daughters to talk to Rob again.

For some reason this was the first thing that popped into my head as Aggie and I turned a corner on our tour of the Tai Tam Tuk Reservoir and spied a four-foot-long snake apparently dozing on the path just a few yards ahead. Rather than attempt to copy Rob and capture or kill the creature, I shouted at Aggie to stop and quietly observe it for a while.

After about two minutes, my naive, uneducated-in-field-craft wife turned to me. "Do you think it's dead?" she asked.

"Of course it's not, you fool!" It was time for some strong words; there was clear and present danger ahead and I had to protect my family, especially as Aggie wasn't feeling too great.

"Well, what are you going to do? It's not moving."

"I can see that, thank you. It could be sleeping and we don't want to wake it up. Pass me some stones will you?" I had Larry on my back so felt happy to give the orders. She sighed and picked up a couple of pebbles from the path-side. I aimed and threw them at its body. They all missed.

"Can I have some more, please?"

"For goodness' sake." She muttered, but acquiesced. I lobbed the next batch with more aplomb and scored a couple of direct hits.

"It's still not moving. I think it's dead."

"I'll be the judge of that." I reached into a tree and pulled out a long, dry stick. Advancing slowly, stamping my feet to make as much noise as possible, I jabbed towards the snake's head in the hope of waking it up and forcing it to scarper. I noticed Aggie following close behind me.

"Get back!" I shouted.

"But you've got Larry on your back—how come he's allowed to get close to it?" She was being a bit clever now.

After a couple of light pokes, the serpent still hadn't so much as twitched. I wacked it, hard. Still nothing.

Aggie stepped forward and peered over the beast.

"Sam, it's got a bloody big hole in its head."

Ah, yes, so it had. We continued on our way in silence.

The aim of the walk was to do a long loop, starting and finishing at Parkview, scene of the Kissel murder. We were having a little difficulty with the map, which wasn't clear at all, being nothing like the good old British Ordnance Survey. The last part of the journey was meant to be roughly flat, or at least slightly inclined at most, but we soon found ourselves heading up Violet Hill, a pleasantly named slope but a bitch to climb with a child on your back. It was boiling hot, and we were both sweating rivers.

"Wait for me, Sam! I'm finding it hard to breathe." Blimey—how unfit is she? I thought. I took her pack and we slowed the pace, but still each step was a challenge for her. Every few seconds she'd launch into a whopping cough and buckle over, hands holding onto a tree for support.

"Are you sure we're going the right way?" she pleaded. But there was only one way now, and so we continued our trudge up. At the top of Violet Hill was a concrete pillar that was a triangulation point—the Ordnance Survey would have been proud—against which Aggie now collapsed in a heap.

For some reason I have a knack of taking photos of Aggie when she least wants it. I don't do it out of anything other than keen interest in my wife, but I have made countless errors in terms of ill-judged photography. This was one. As the camera snapped her prone body, she looked up at me and launched into what can only be described as a rant.

Looking at the photo now puts the situation in a whole new light. That night she was still finding it difficult to breathe and her rattling cough was becoming worse. She still insisted on going to work the next day, but after about five minutes her colleague gave her a green surgical mask to wear out of a fear of infection. That was the final straw, and she headed to see the doctor.

An hour later and she was in hospital having numerous tests. The quacks were worried that she had developed either TB or, worse still, lung cancer, and were subjecting her to a barrage of checks to properly identify the illness. This meant that she had to stay in hospital overnight while they performed a lung biopsy, which was all quite worrying. The hospital room, high up in a green glass tower, had a superb view of

Happy Valley, and the canteen was more like a high-end Chinese restaurant—they were the best Singapore noodles I had ever had in Hong Kong, which, although laudable, was not much of a silver lining.

It was a sad end to the year.

"The doctor said it is probably caused by air pollution. If it is, you realise that we will have to go back home?" As I left her for the night, ahead of her operation the following morning, it became clear that, just as our social life and my job situation were starting to come good, our stay in Hong Kong was perhaps not going to be too lengthy after all.

EIGHTEEN

....

In early 2003 a sixty-four-year-old doctor arrived in Hong Kong to attend a wedding. He had travelled from southern China where he had been treating victims of a decidedly nasty flu-like infection that had so far killed several dozen people. Despite having fallen ill a week before with similar symptoms to those he was treating, he had felt well enough to knock around town for a while, staying in the fancy Metropole Hotel and sightseeing with his brother-in-law. The next day he felt worse and went to hospital, but it was too late. He died ten days later.

Unfortunately for Hong Kong, Dr Liu had become the Special Administrative Region's first victim of SARS. Over the next four months a further one thousand, seven hundred and fifty-four people became infected with the disease, many of them medical professionals treating the infected. One ill man alone managed to pass on SARS to ninety-nine hospital workers, including seventeen medical students, who probably highly regretted turning up to class that day. In total two hundred and ninety-nine people in Hong Kong died, including Dr Liu's brother-in-law and several of the his fellow Metropole guests—one of whom flew to Taiwan and unwittingly spread the disease there too.

What made SARS so devastating for Hong Kong was not its death rate, which was high at around seventeen percent of those infected— appearing on the list somewhere between bubonic plague and anthrax—

but because of the economic impact. As soon as the virus struck the territory went into meltdown. Expat families fled, Chinese locals fled, as many people as possible fled, all seeking healthier climes. Tourists disappeared, and Hong Kong businesses were banned from travelling overseas, for example to the vast Basel Fair in Switzerland, costing them tens of millions of dollars in lost revenue. It was a categorically destructive incident.

Like many bad experiences though there were some longer lasting benefits. As neighbour Vivian described it, "Overnight everyone became more health conscious. You know, I hadn't seen anyone wearing a face mask before SARS, but since then people know that if they're ill they put one on. They even started disinfecting the elevator call buttons and putting up a little sign to tell you. And don't you even think about sneezing in an elevator, you'll not be popular. It's so much cleaner now, but SARS was so horrible no one wants to see that again."

Such was the continued obsession with SARS that the news channels filled their schedules with nothing else at the first sign of bird flu. One winter morning we noticed in the morning paper that three chickens were found to have died from a flu strain at a market. We switched on the TV to see being broadcast, rather unnecessarily in my mind, twenty-four hour footage of seventeen thousand hens being dumped into tall green wheelie bins and gassed to death. No health, no mercy.

Luckily enough, the tests on Aggie were negative for SARS, or anything remotely similar, and she was soon back at home. What they did reveal was an autoimmune disease called sarcoidosis that was, for the most part, untreatable. This may have been because no one knew what on earth it was, which no doubt explained why, apart from a short course of tablets, the main cure appeared to be rest, and plenty of it. This suited her, as whatever it was she had developed was making her extremely tired.

I, on the other hand, felt guiltily fine, apart from some seasonal excess. I awoke on New Year's Day with the customary hangover, mouth as dry as a Sahara sand storm and head as thick as treacle, having welcomed in January with Tom and a few of his cronies. I had left them in the early hours as they tucked into yet more flaming cocktails, their singleton life outshining my responsibility-laden one with quite some exuberance.

Poor Aggie meanwhile had spent the night in bed, dosed up on antibiotics and cough medicine so strong it was probably outlawed in the UK, with just a glass of warm Riesling for comfort. She only stirred when the expansive midnight fireworks began a few hundred yards from her bedroom window.

Yet the Dragon Lady spirit was firing in her. Safe in the knowledge that she was not carrying a communicable disease, and determined not to let it ruin her social life, she foolishly insisted on spending New Year's Day on Lantau Island with Chlöe and Cameron. Lantau is far larger than Hong Kong Island, a mountainous outpost to the west and home to Disneyland and the airport. It is thoroughly under-populated compared to the rest of the territory, partly because of the multitude of its mountains which are highly popular with walkers. It also has a picturesque coast that is known for its beaches, holiday houses, and wild cows that march along, disrupting cars and picnickers but generally just munching their fill.

It may be a rural getaway, but it was also miles away. After riding in a taxi, then a ferry, then a bus, we finally reached the famous Cheung Sha beach, at the south centre of the island. This wonderfully wide patch of sand is known for its South African restaurant, which made Cameron and Chlöe feel thoroughly at home. Quite an international gathering had been assembled; half a dozen countries were represented, and with plenty of little kiddies for Larry to play with. Best of all was a beautiful dog named Thelma, who was a rescue dog that lived with two boisterous young children and could therefore put up with Larry's vigorous version of stroking. It was a gorgeous setting on a fairly empty beach, with a few hardy swimmers now the temperature was finally a solid cool, and deep greenery stretching up behind us. Larry, when not playing with Thelma, liked nothing more than to sit there picking up handfuls of sand, tasting it intermittently. ("Yep, that's still sandy. Let's try that again.") Had it not been for Aggie's weak lungs and Larry's dinner awaiting, we could quite happily have sat there all afternoon getting gently sozzled and watching the sun set. Not for the first time did I say to myself that Hong Kong felt like a holiday.

Happily, as January progressed, Aggie's health improved quite dramatically, and although she was still knackered the entire time, she continued to deny the sarcoidosis the chance to restrict her. So at the end of the month, and with the weather really quite fresh, she started swimming to reclaim some measure of fitness.

It was quite refreshing for her to be in the water, since by this time we were now suffering at least one hundred percent humidity on land. The humidity was really quite unbearable, and going for a run made me wetter than a haddock. With the apartment sodden—the salt cellar had long since clumped together into a useless gunge—I was dispatched to the main electronics store of Hong Kong, Fortress, to purchase another dehumidifier. My mission was hastened when we discovered black and dark green mould had started to grow right across our wardrobe contents. The effect on our skin meanwhile was to make us feel a bit 'tacky.' As Aggie noted, "Forget 'cleanse, tone, and moisturise'...here I just cleanse, tone, and step outside."

It wasn't just the humidity that wasn't welcome. For days on end the sky had been highly fusty, so much so that Kowloon, although only a couple of miles away at most, was hardly visible. Yet when we looked up high we could see patches of blue with white clouds scattered about. In other words, it wasn't just a general fog, it was pollution. Surprisingly—and thankfully—the onset of this thickset pollution didn't make much difference to Aggie's lungs. It did make everyone a bit paranoid about their children, but Larry didn't seem to be suffering either.

The appearance of all this disgusting air was a not a surprise, given Hong Kong still hadn't agreed to accept World Health Organisation standards on the testing of air quality. Instead they had arbitrarily assured the population that the air was fine. Well, maybe in comparison with the Mainland. The cities there, like Beijing, had pollution that had to be seen to be believed. It was even rumoured that the air quality monitors in the Chinese capital's US Embassy had broken on one especially bad day, as they had choked on the too-thick particulate matter. An airline pilot I once met told me that you can see China from several hundred miles away as you fly in, appearing as a thick yellowy-brown haze that hovers above the country.

Here in Hong Kong it wasn't that bad, or indeed as serious as the pea-souper smogs that afflicted London in the 1950s. But ultimately all the expats here—and plenty of local Chinese—would have had to make a call as to whether the pollution, such as it was, was a price worth paying to live here.

NINETEEN

···

Another potential fly in the ointment of happy family life was the school system. We had been warned time and time again how difficult it would be to find a slot for Larry. Neighbour Vivian had even called us around for a special chat, with a pre-prepared list of schools to look at, fuelled by a mountain of biscuits large enough to feed a hundred kids.

"Oh my God, you haven't started looking yet? You must be crazy. Now, here is a list of schools for you to consider..." and with that she launched into a monologue on which was good, which was bad, and what the gossip was with each one.

Pah, we thought. But after a couple of months I idly gave one rec-ommended establishment a ring to hear that the intake for Larry was already full—for the next four years. Needless to say we quickly set about finding a school for him.

If you could actually find a school for your offspring, then Hong Kong was a great place to be. According to one global league table for educational excellence, Hong Kong lay in third place, above the UK in sixth. This disparity between the two might seem strange given that local Hong Kong education had been modelled on the English system until only a few years previously. This was when Beijing decided that the best way to encourage national togetherness was to start brainwashing the population early, and so stopped Hong Kong state schools following the UK.

With expat parents not wanting to send their children to local Beijing-directed schools, the international establishments were all full to bursting. This did not stop them taking the registration fees of anxious parents, which was a nice little earner for them. This came into sharp focus on one visit we had. I had telephoned a particular school to ask about Larry attending primary school there—in four years' time, remember—and they had advised me to submit his registration form as soon as possible, at a cost of several thousand dollars.

"Shouldn't we wait until we have visited?"

"Well, you could," replied the nasal admissions woman, "but the list is almost full, and you don't want to miss out, I assure you." So we paid the money and arranged to have a look around at the earliest opportunity, which was a few weeks hence.

The school, housed in a lovingly renovated building, really was quite something. The difference with my former places of study couldn't have been starker. For a start in that the children were actually learning and not trying to smash things in the corner. There didn't seem to be any evidence of someone trying to burn it down (which happened at every school I attended, coincidentally) and there were no fag butts outside the front door.

We finished the tour in high spirits; Larry would definitely be happy here, and we said so to the headmaster—an Englishman with a face reminiscent of a tubby scout leader. He gave us a quizzical look.

"Is your son actually on the waiting list?" Yes, we replied, we paid our money. "Let me have a quick check," and with that he left the room.

Five minutes later a Chinese woman in a swishing red dress and with curly black hair stood in the doorway.

"I think there is a misunderstanding," she announced. I stood up.

"What do you mean?"

"Well unfortunately I do not think your child will be coming to our school." This may have been something my own parents had been used to as they tried to hawk me around to anywhere that would have me, but Larry surely couldn't have broken the law yet.

"He is 179th on the waiting list," she explained, "and there are only twenty places. So you see it is better if you look elsewhere."

We were stupefied. It had only been a few weeks since we had registered him, so what on earth was going on? I complained that they had taken a hefty and non-refundable fee and wasted our morning, and all for nothing. But she had an indisputable answer for that.

"Oh no, it is not for nothing. Of course there is a chance one hundred and fifty-nine children may not turn up."

Luckily we had had more luck with his nursery, where he was fine for now. After he had spent a few months at a playgroup we had decided to move him on to a bit more of a structured day, so had sent him to Tutortime, an American nursery that had excellent reviews and, more importantly, a place. Run by a young Colorado teacher with spikey blonde hair and a voice straight out of the nearest gravel pit, it was mainly full of children who were Chinese to look at, but Brits and Americans to hear. They also had a refreshingly positive attitude to competition and factual learning that was totally opposite to the ridiculous trend in the British state system.

I discovered this, plus the background of some of Larry's classmates, when I attended the annual sports day. By now I was playing a healthy amount of sport each week, far more than I had been in the UK at any rate. Hockey a couple of times a week, a game of tennis, and a slow run were acting as a good counterweight to my socialising with Tom, and a change of scene from my work with Craig. I was consequently looking forward to a bit of sports day action.

It was, however, hard to understand what a two-year-old youngster had to offer the world of running, athletics, and egg & spoon races, but I can tell you that it was actually quite a lot, at least in terms of effort. Larry and I waited for an age outside his school for the coach to come. He was already dressed in his sports kit—a dainty concoction of yellow polo shirt and matching hat—but such was the cold that he had to wear a thick coat on top, somewhat spoiling the effect. As soon as we were aboard he fell asleep, proving that the only pre-tournament nerves were mine. We were driving towards one of Hong Kong's largest sports grounds, which in itself was a clear statement on how seriously Tutortime took its competition. Despite this I was sure all Larry could think of was why on earth his father was taking him on a bus.

School had organised a series of events lined up for the kids, some bland, some ridiculous. The first involved having to boringly run across some hoops. The next was to follow a wavy line on the floor whilst carrying a beanbag. But the football stand was left field. Rather than dribble the ball to the end, Larry had to carry it in a fluorescent towel. What on earth was that all about? He didn't care in the least, and just dropped the towel and kicked the ball as hard as he could. It was good to make Dad run a bit, he must have thought as I repeatedly jogged over to the next door event to collect the ball.

Then it was big race time, the race to end all races. The 'carry ping pong balls for twenty yards in a small net normally designed to take tropical fish out of their tanks and then drop the ball in a colour-coded box' competition was upon us. The teacher, a lanky American graduate with an angular face and tufty, student hair, made the kids line up at the start. The children fidgeted, the fathers strained at the start. I made eye contact with the man next to me; no matter that he was a thoroughly nice bloke from Manchester, I was still going to take him down. I had entered the world of Competitive Dad.

We were off. I showed off my athleticism by accidentally stepping in front of the Mancunian next to me, giving us a second head start. Larry's legs pumped, his eyes fixed on the ball-in-net. But then disaster! The ball flew out, hitting the track and rolling off out of reach. I dove, quickly grabbing it up and popping it back in the net, but by then we had been overtaken by a kid in a ripped cream anorak. Spurred on by the shame, we reached the yellow box in record time, but in the brouhaha Larry forget what he was meant to do.

"Put it in the hole!" I suggested, as calmly as you might expect.

Job done, we raced back to the box of balls and started the process again. This time Larry dropped the net in the hole too, which really slowed us down but made him chuckle mischievously. Then we returned for yet another go. Six, seven, eight...after the tenth run I felt a bit out of breath but Larry kept us going. Until we looked up and realised that we were the only ones racing. We had whooped them! Well, actually, all the other competitors had moved on to the next stand.

The combination of sport and competition may have been a constructive one, even with me as a father, but one potential downside to being educated in China was the potential to fall into speaking Chinglish. This was a phenomenon that was rife across China, and which no one in authority gave any indication of noticing, apart from the well-educated Hong Kong Establishment. The concept was simple; the world's two most spoken languages were merged into an almost understandable middle ground. What was unexpected to anyone who had not encountered it before, such as myself, was how absolutely ridiculous many of the translations into English were.

This fact had not gone unnoticed by the Beijing Government. In a land where face was everything, fluffing the language was not admired. It was in this spirit that Chinese officials carried out campaigns to reduce Chinglish in preparation for the 2008 Summer Olympics in Beijing and the Expo 2010 in Shanghai.

Soon after the International Olympic Committee selected Beijing in 2001, the Beijing Tourism Bureau established a tipster hotline for Chinglish errors on signs, such as emergency exits at the Beijing airport reading 'No entry on peacetime.' In 2007, the Beijing Speaks Foreign Languages Program reported they had worked out four thousand, six hundred and twenty-four pieces of standard English translations to substitute the Chinglish ones on signs around the city. For instance, 'Be careful, road slippery' instead of 'To take notice of safe: The slippery are very crafty.' The program chairman Chen Lin was reported as saying "We want everything to be correct. Grammar, words, culture, everything. Beijing will have thousands of visitors coming. We don't want anyone laughing at us."

Quite predictably, foreign writers spent acres of ink commenting on the appearance of Chinglish at the Shanghai 2010 Expo, where banners advertised the Three Georges Dam exhibit rather than the Three Gorges, and asked what the reason was for these mistranslations. It may not be too PC to chuckle at Chinese translators getting it wrong, especially as my Mandarin could launch a thousand laughs for a start, but so many of the errors were so simple that even if they had shown them to just one native English speaker then they could have been resolved. As one journalist remarked, "It truly is bizarre that so many organizations in China are willing to chisel English translations into stone, paint them on signs, print them on business cards, and expose them permanently to the world without making any effort to check whether they are right."

Sadly the standard of most Hong Kongers' English, especially the younger ones, was still so good that Chinglish rarely appeared in all its glory. That is where the internet came in. Of all the mistranslations to raise a smile—and restaurant menus, according to the online forums, seemed to be a rich source of them, such as 'Braised enterovirus in Clay Pot' (or 'stuffed sausage' as it should have been)—the champion had to be a bootleg version of Star Wars: Episode III - Revenge of the Sith. Or, as it was translated, Star War - The Third Gathers: Backstroke of the West.

As noted by the guy who found the copy and then published it online, "Amazingly enough, the beginning scroll is mistranslated even though the words are right there on the screen." When an anonymous doomed fighter pilot announced in the opening scene that, "They're all over me" the subtitles come up with "He is in my behind." Obi Wan followed this by philosophically announcing "Like, reach the man, Good good good let us counter-attacking" before chastising R2D2 with the stern words "R2, do you is fucking." Not to be outdone, Count Dooku got tough with "You are a sacrifice article that I cut up rough now", before General Grievous received some bad news about the two Jedi: "Superior, they have escaped a day after the fair." A little later Annakin ecumenically announced that he was "Just made by the Presbyterian Church" (aka the Jedi Council—probably a lawsuit waiting to happen) before wishing Obi Wan "Ratio tile, the wish power are together with you" ("May the Force be with you" of course). There were plenty of surreal references to elephants and the Milky Way too, as well as a "dead period", and a "flock of to fish". Fittingly, the last line, given by Darth Vader upon hearing that his beloved Padme was dead, was not "Noooooooooooooo—" but the more accurate, yet totally less passionate, "Do not want."

TWENTY

....

I thought something might be in the air when I went to the super-market to find the whole place awash with tangerines. These weren't loose, but were still suspended from the little tangerine bushes that had been placed at the entrance and along the aisles, their pots wrapped in gold and red. Even I, not the world's most observant shopper, couldn't fail to realise that these decorations were not normal for Hong Kong. It was just another difference between supermarkets here and back home. There were similarities of course, and most stores included Anglo-Saxon staples like Hershey's chocolate, Marmite, and Walkers crisps; some even had Waitrose products in them, much to the relief of many a homesick Brit.

There were, however, stunning areas of difference, especially around the produce served. For instance, fish heads. As in, whole salmon heads carefully removed from the body, placed in cling film, and sold as seen. Uncooked chicken feet were another item not normally seen in Hamp-stead's Tesco, and neither were a whole raft of fruits and vegetables that were new to us. Choi sum (Chinese cabbage: very tasty, especially fried with garlic), Asian pears (not too bad, but why not stick with Western pears?), and bitter melon (won't make that mistake again) were all tried, unlike the fowl feet which didn't tempt me after that first taste all those years ago.

It wasn't just supermarkets that had different food stock. The more Chinese parts of Hong Kong Island had many a shop selling Chinese delicacies of every type. Dried fish swim-bladders, hacked-off sharks fins, and edible birds' nests were all for sale, along with more obscure pieces of wildlife that were special ingredients for Chinese medicine recipes.

Traditional Chinese Medicine, or TCM as it is widely known, is huge in Hong Kong, as might be imagined. Even work insurance policies allow a visit to a traditional Chinese doctor, and it was common for us to hear of people shuttling between Western and TCM cures looking for that extra slice of health.

Effective it might have been, but TCM had some pretty alternative ingredients. One shop just off the Midlevels escalator was a true depository of the weird cure, at least in Western eyes. Women, are you suffering from irregular menstruation, dizziness, and palpitations? Try "asses' glue" - it nourishes the lungs, apparently. Monkey's visceral organs: useful for the removal of excessive sputum, and dried geckos—literally whole, dried lizards—are good for strengthening the liver and curing impotence. There wasn't a lot from the animal kingdom that the shop didn't stock.

Anyway, back to the supermarket decorations. Tangerine bushes and associated banners soon started popping up in streets and in residential blocks too, heralding yet another festival: Chinese New Year.

Here's a question for you: which is the world's largest migration? You might think it the numberless wildebeest of the Serengeti, surging past crocodile ambushes and ahead of snapping lion jaws; or perhaps the monarch butterfly, millions of them filling the forests of Mexico each year.

You would, however, be wrong. The biggest movement of beings each year, at least above the multicellular level, is the movement of Chinese for their New Year. Every January or February, depending on the moon, hundreds of millions of people make their way around the Moth-

erland, heading back to their birth villages to spend time with their family. Migratory workers form the majority of the numbers, and their favourite means of transport is rail, so the train authorities have a heck of a
task in coordinating the timetable to make sure that three billion rail
journeys jammed into just forty days start and end on time. Considering
that in Britain the First Great Western company routinely fails to make
their poxy little service run according to schedule at the best of times, as
I had found out repeatedly to my cost and sanity when travelling to see
my friends in the West Country, a magnitude of organisation like this
would be enough to give First Great Western's planners an instant coro-
nary.

In Hong Kong though, Chinese New Year, or 'Chunyun', was char-
acterised not by migration but by money.

"I suppose you know about lai see?" said neighbour Vivian one evening over dinner; apart from providing us with the latest gossip on the
Indian neighbours below, she had cooked us one of her favourite
Shanghainese dishes, a spicy chicken composition that was so hot it nearly made us cry. New Year was fast approaching and we were feeling un-
prepared, so we were keen to know what we should and shouldn't be
doing.

"It's where you hand out money to people, with those little red envelopes that you see in all the shops at the moment. Aggie, you should give
them to everyone that works for you. One year this girl I know, she
didn't bother, and no one made her a cup of coffee the rest of the year!
And this other girl..."

Being British, handing out money, face to face, really was a challeng-
ing concept. We supposed it was like a Christmas tip for the paperboy,
but on a more organised scale. As I only had one colleague, who being
Australian didn't really fit into the whole New Year custom, I was feeling
quite left out, until Vivian clarified by pointing out that the Grand Panorama staff needed an envelope too. This was slightly disturbing as there
were dozens of staff, and if each one required a decent tip this could

quickly accumulate. Suffice it to say I was glad of the inherent stinginess in my Yorkshire ancestry.

"Oh honey, don't worry about that. It's the thought that counts so you only need to give them twenty dollars or so. And they'll receive loads of lai see packets so they'll make plenty." This was very cheap news indeed.

Over the New Year weekend itself we were all ill with flu, so were unable to get out and enjoy all the celebrations. Not that there was much to see in the first place, as all the Chinese spent the four days at home with their families. Many, if not most, of the shops were shut, and even the old bastions of expat life like the clubs were mainly shut to give their employees a holiday. Once the weekend was over, and we were all on our feet again, the three of us set out across the Grand Panorama estate armed with plenty of envelopes, all of which contained brand new notes as was the custom. As we met each of the staff we did a little bow and passed over the money with two hands, announcing "Kung hei fat choi" ('Happy New Year' in Cantonese), which of course made us feel quite local. Vivian may have been telling the truth about the amount, but it didn't stop Sister Wan, the car park attendant, from looking like I'd decapitated her pet dog when she opened up the packet. Luckily we didn't have a car to be 'accidentally scratched'—I could see what she was thinking behind those ungrateful milk-bottle glasses. At least Sister Yi, still wrapped up tight in her thick jumper, looked happy; well, as happy as her continually mournful eyes would allow.

Aggie had to deliver at work too, so she loaded up her handbag with crisp new twenties in shiny red envelopes, and proceeded to dish them out. Strictly speaking they should only have been given to those more junior than her, but this led to a difficulty with the secretaries. Many of these, at Aggie's work at least, were the wives of wealthy men so only really went to work to pass the time. So the question was, would it have been an insult to give them the equivalent of £1.80? Yes, probably, came the response from some of the more seasoned gweilos, so Aggie restrained herself to giving only to those without a rich sugar daddy.

In terms of work, January wasn't the best for me. Craig had been awarded the contract for directing and presenting an environmental documentary on plastic waste in the ocean which would take him away for several months, and while I was excited for him—and, to be honest, jealous of him lounging about the south of France and Fiji—it did mean that my short-lived volunteer work was at an end. Added to this was the fact that my proposed position with the bank had been canned due to staff cut-backs, which was an absolute annoyance. Luckily I had a few more potential irons in the employment fire, but they were few and far between and I was worried they would melt before I had a chance to land them.

After I finished on the phone to Craig, Aggie and I went for a mind-cleansing walk up to the Peak; well, a taxi ride, because her lungs were still not working properly. Aggie had suffered a bit of a relapse and had been forced to spend the last few days in bed, too weak to move and coughing like a banshee. We stood in silence at the railing, overlooking the millions of lights that blinked for a city that, we worried, might not be our home for much longer.

"It's not been as smooth as we thought it would, has it?"

We had had our ups and downs since we arrived, for sure, but there was a feeling now between us that we had reached a crossroads. Aggie's illness may not have been caused by Hong Kong, but it was definitely not making it better. And me being unemployed was absolutely not part of the plan; despite the excitement of getting to know Hong Kong I was really not that happy with life without a steady job. We agreed that we would give it to the end of March, and if I hadn't found a willing employer, and Aggie wasn't substantially better, then we would pack our bags and return home.

TWENTY-ONE

....

Y ou want Chinese wife?" asked the taxi driver as we sped over
the Admiralty overpass.

"Er, no, I have a British wife," I replied, fairly surprised
that my trip to hockey was developing into a motorised version of Blind
Date. The driver twisted in his seat to give me a wink and an unshaven
grin.

"Chinese woman, she very good for you."

"That may be so, but I think one's enough for now."

"So you no want Chinese wife?"

"Thanks, but no thanks." The driver went quiet, and the taxi lurched
around another corner before settling into a steady hum along a straight
bit of road.

A minute later his back snapped straight as he thought of something
else. "But you be careful, yes, because if Chinese woman want you she
take you. Chinese women very smart."

I wasn't sure that I would have been a catch for anyone other than
my present spouse, but many a Westerner has fallen for the local women
in Hong Kong. Stories abound of Western couples arriving together but
leaving separately, the man invariably finding himself intoxicated by a
new Asian belle. Katie, an American teacher who I met watching the
rugby one night, explained how difficult it could be as a non-local woman here.

"So many male Westerners fall for Asian girls when they arrive, so it's really difficult to find a man for more than just a night. I tell all my single girlfriends: if you want a husband, don't stay in Hong Kong."

A British friend of a friend, Rebecca, explained it further.

"At some of the bars I've been to I've had a man come up to me within literally a couple of minutes and ask me if I want to go home with him. When I say no he'll just walk off and find another girl. It's quite depressing really because all the Western men just get it into their heads that girls are for the night and not for a relationship."

Yet not all expats were up for a long-term bond. One place where everyone was up for a good transient time was on a junk trip. According to the Encyclopaedia Britannica, the junk is a "classic Chinese sailing vessel of ancient unknown origin, still in wide use." To every expat in Hong Kong they were party boats extraordinaire. They were, quite simply, the best place to drink in Hong Kong. Most of the Taipans—the British companies out here, like Jardines, Swires, Hong Kong Land, Dairy Farm, Standard Chartered, and so on—owned one or two, and they were in constant use by employees both young and old.

Many a junk trip turned boozy, but the worst, not surprisingly, were the stag dos. One close friend of mine from the UK, who for legal reasons shall remain nameless, emigrated to Asia on the Monday and was in Hong Kong for a bachelor party by the Friday. After a heavy first night, Saturday morning dawned and the junk started filling up with hungover young men of a variety of different backgrounds and nationalities. One thing they did have in common was a heady enthusiasm to make the groom-to-be have a hard-drinking time.

After a short outward-bound journey they anchored at a sheltered bay and let the tomfoolery begin. The injuries started quite soon after. Leaping from the roof, but landing on the deck rather than the sea: broken ribs. Slipping over on excessively spilled beer: torn arm ligaments. Walking into a low beam: cut eye. It was, to all intents and purposes, a typical rough and tumble affair, anaesthetized by enough drink to start a chain of off-licences. Then the gate-crashers arrived.

"Hi over there! Are you having a party?" Two girls, around twenty years old and dressed in the type of minimalist bikinis called 'dental floss' by the ever-descriptive Brazilians, were calling over from their mega-speedboat.

"Can we come over? Sounds like fun!"

My friend, being able to somewhat take his drink, had spotted this and was desperately trying to tell them it wasn't a good idea. But his cries went unanswered as the girls, accompanied by an equally buff man of a similar age no doubt wearing Vilebrequin shorts, dived into the sea and swam over.

The expressions of these young Gatsby-esque creatures can only be imagined as they hauled themselves onto the junk. There in front of them were fifteen men stood in a circle around the stag, chanting something prehistoric, and surrounded by broken bottles, beer, and blood. No matter how you looked at it, this was not going to end well.

The young lad looked like he had taken a vault over a wall only to discover it was a two-hundred-foot cliff. He had no time to dwell on the matter though, because exactly three seconds later he had been dragged into the circle too, whereupon a satanic cocktail was thrust into his hands and he was loudly encouraged to imbibe from a shoe.

The girls were left aside while their male companion was dealt with, but after he had started retching they were considerately asked what they wanted to drink. Before an answer could be uttered, pints of beer tinged with vodka were handed over; one sip was enough for one of them to start shouting over to their own boat. Unfortunately "Daddy! Daddy! DADDY!" couldn't hear them.

Within six minutes they had all thrown up, adding yet more bodily fluids to the deck, but then they were in such a bad state that there was nothing to do but relax. Eventually, after they had been gone quite a while, Daddy started to worry and so sent a tender over to collect them.

History doesn't record the reception they had when back on board, but it was probably true to say the rest of their evening was a write-off.

Aggie and I had been invited on a junk trip by Cameron and Chlöe, but given that it was a cold February, and most of us were married with kids, it was a slightly more sober affair than those we might have enjoyed a few years before. There was plenty of vomit, but this was mainly down to the high waves as we chugged through the sea towards the island of Po Toi.

This is the most southerly point of the territory and a somewhat overlooked member of its many islands. It appeared quite different from many of the others, being under-populated and under-forested in equal measure. The coast was marked by a hiking trail that was an unremarkable mixture of the flat and the slightly undulating, which Cameron and Chlöe enthusiastically led us around. The path builders had tried to enliven the walking experience by placing the occasional signpost indicating a local wonder alongside it, but as the highlight of these was a natural stone edifice called 'Palm Rock'—because it looked somewhat like a human hand—the enlivenment was not an unqualified success.

Still, it was good to get the legs moving, blow the sea-sickness away, and rustle up a fine appetite. We finished our walk at a wonderful restaurant, which was actually the only one on the island as far as we could see. Ming Kee overlooks a mussel-shaped bay, which, over the course of our sauntering lunch, filled up with yachts coming over to enjoy the hearty seafood. With a concrete floor, plastic chairs, and serviced by a public lavatory that lay between a diesel generator and a rubbish tip, it was never going to win any awards for luxury dining. But the chilli prawns, salt and pepper squid, whole baked fish—and, for the carnivores, boneless sweet and sour pork—was Cantonese comfort food at its best. The waitresses spoke English with semi-Oxford accents too, which was a surprise until we heard the story, oft repeated at lunch, of how they were educated at private schools in the UK on the restaurant's proceeds. Reflecting the close relations that local families generally enjoyed, they both now worked in Central but came over to the island each weekend to help their parents.

Something else discussed at lunch were the recent nuptials of a man known simply as the Beast of Wanchai. No one at the table seemed to know who on earth this person was, other than being a rapacious devourer of woman and wine in equal amount. His name had been first mentioned by Tom over a beer in Soho, along with a large dollop of awe. It sounded like he was describing one of the Classical Gods rather than a habitually hammered womaniser, so Tom would have been perhaps surprised to hear the latest tale of the Beast. For what was of interest this time was not his latest bender, or his ability to track down four air stewardesses with only one bed and a lonesome evening to fill, but the fact that he was joining the marriage club. And, it was remarked, he wasn't settling down with a local, but with a solid English rose from Gloucestershire whose cheeks were as fresh as a bunny's tail.

"You see, it is possible for British girls to find a husband here," said the woman next to me, who had of course found her beau back home before moving here. The thing is, this appeared very much to be the exception, and no matter where the Beast ended up, the majority of relationships started by Western men in Hong Kong were with Asian girls.

It was obviously not one-way traffic. Western men weren't doing all the running—Asian girls were on the hunt too. For the Filipina maids that spent their Sunday afternoons in the bars of Wanchai looking for drunk Brits or Aussies it was not hard to see what the attraction was, i.e. leaving domestic service and having a relatively wealthy man look after them, no matter how fat, bald, or windy he was. What was perhaps more questionable was why many Hong Kong women sought out fellas from London or New York. An anthropologist would be able to give you many a reason why the female of the species looks for mates outside of her own gene pool, but here it seemed that the answer was more prosaic; there just weren't enough single, local men to go around. Whereas in China there were millions of extra men thanks to high levels of female infanticide, here in Hong Kong the ratio was switched. There were, by some estimates, more than two hundred thousand excess women. This was less of a direct physical threat to society compared to having tens of millions of extra men roaming around—single women don't tend to form gangs and launch rebellions—but it did make finding a boyfriend or husband a different type of challenge to more gender-balanced countries.

Yet for some this numerical imbalance was a side issue in explaining marriage trends. New Moon, as always, was quick to explain her own reason for why Hong Kong women didn't always marry local men. We were enjoying a lesson on body parts, which somehow moved onto dating.

"Many Hong Kong men prefer Mainland wives because they are quieter and cause fewer problems. Hong Kong women know their mind, and many men do not like this, so they find a Mainlander to marry."

Neighbour Vivian, who probably knew more about the secret lives and agendas of Hong Kong's people than most, agreed.

"These young Mainland girls, they're so beautiful. When they talk to a man they're very coy, all "Yes, yes, whatever you say." But as soon as he turns his back they get all tough, and some of them quite nasty too. They make a good wife for Hong Kong men because they are obedient. Well, that's the theory."

So, many of the local men married Mainlanders. But having listened to how picky some of the Hong Kong women were about their potential spouses it was no surprise that many blokes looked for easier relationships across the border, as New Moon again explained.

"Many Hong Kong women are arrogant and very inflexible. They want the perfect package of a man—good looking, well-educated, with a well-paid job—but they don't realise that this is a very rare thing. Sometimes you have to make compromises in life." No wonder the local fertility rate was so low.

This was the thing about Hong Kong women; they were certainly strong-willed. This was reflected by the attitude of the numerous forceful females that we saw, women in business so ferocious that they had a moniker all to themselves. Aggie's work was dominated by these so-called Dragon Ladies, women not of iron or steel, but tungsten, and woe betide if you crossed them.

Talking of work, my own road to employment was still not going so well, despite continuing to network at a high-octane pace. One problem I was finding was that many of the jobs required fluent Mandarin. My lessons with New Moon were going well, and I was filling out page after page of my exercise book practising my characters, but I was nowhere near being able to conduct business in the language.

It began to look like I had an unenviable choice: to accept a job here in Hong Kong totally at odds with my career to date, or to look for an exciting role abroad where business Mandarin wasn't required. To say the least, this was not exactly what either of us had been hoping for. So I decided to ask Sid, one of Tom's mates who managed to combine the blunt, intelligent, and almost angry charm of Dr David Starkey with the networking ability of Bill Clinton.

"The thing is," said Sid, "you're looking in the wrong place. Have you thought about Singapore? It's not too bad there, and you don't need anything but English." He sipped his coffee and pushed his glasses back on to the bridge of his nose. A couple of finely dressed Chinese business women clip-clopped past, window browsing the ten thousand dollar handbags that the Landmark shopping centre, bang in the heart of Central, seemed to specialise in.

"Well, not really. I don't think being a four hour plane ride away would be too conducive to a happy home life."

"Nonsense! Plenty of people commute to and from Singapore."

If you were to ask an inhabitant of Hong Kong or Singapore about the other then you would most likely receive an unflattering comment. Ever since Hong Kong was founded, some twenty-two years after Singapore's founder Sir Stamford Raffles started the process of turning a tiger-infested swamp into a South-East Asian entrepôt of extraordinary note, the two former colonies have been competing to outdo each other. Hong Kongers invariably deride Singapore as "Disneyland with the death penalty" in reference to its pseudo-perfection and its habit of executing those that cross the line. Singaporeans on the other hand think of their northern neighbour as being "dirty, polluted, and too close to China for comfort."

But Singapore had some clear advantages for us. There were more plentiful school places for Larry, less crowded streets, and, obliquely, the attraction of one of the world's best zoos complete with white tigers enough for both Siegfried and Roy. Another significant benefit of Singapore was the superior air quality there; sneezes didn't leave a trail of black on one's handkerchief, unlike in Hong Kong. And although there was no obvious or stated medical link between Aggie's sarcoidosis and the pollution, it may have been a good thing to move not just me but the whole family there.

As we finished our coffee I began to see Sid's point of view. I did have some friends in Singapore whose sofa I could sleep on while looking for gainful employment, so it was a possibility. And if Aggie was unable to relocate—which was doubtful at least in the short term as she had only just started her job—then the family would only be four short hours away. Yet it was still a different country...Hmm, it was something to think about at least.

Sid was undergoing a career change of his own. He was, unusually, retraining to be a barrister. I say unusually because there seemed to be a great deal of apprehension about the future of Hong Kong's independent legal system. It was far from clear whether British lawyers would have much of a future, thanks to increasing worries about Beijing's impact on the Hong Kong judicial process. There had been a hell of a hullabaloo about this after a retiring judge had expressed his fears over keeping Mainland China's influence away from the courts; although the official line was that he was speaking nonsense, whispers at networking drinks—I always ended up speaking to lawyers at these things for some reason, perhaps why I was still unemployed—intonated that all was not well in the law here, at least for the long term prognosis.

Having said that, the legal profession was still growing. Despite disquiet, the law in Hong Kong was still vastly more trusted than that on the Mainland. It was widely reported that the number of foreign lawyers here had doubled over the last few years, spurred by Hong Kong's booming economy and its role as the gateway to China. Being a common law territory made it easier for British, American, and Antipodean solicitors to make the move, and they were doing so in droves. There were, however, not that many new barristers being called to the local bar; Sid was the exception.

It was a cold, grey, and frankly British February morning as I headed to court for Sid's ceremony, the kind of day when coats were brought out for a rare appearance and the rain was for once not refreshing. The High Court was, to my surprise, not in some imposing old building with arches and columns and all things hierarchical. It was instead in a faded concrete structure that resembled a 1960s council building in Milton Keynes, hardly in keeping with its role as the highest legal entity in the land. It seemed incongruous that a territory that owed so much to the rule of law would treat its High Court with such architectural disdain. This was, after all, the city that, according to Dr Sun Yat-sen, the man who lead the 1911 overthrow of the last Emperor of China and who is considered by many to be an 'All Chinese Hero', had been built on a working legal system.

"During my brief visit to Hong Kong I recognised the beauty of western architecture, the tidiness of streets, and the stringency of law and order. The effectiveness of their rule of law reminds me that the Westerners should not be looked down as 'barbarians' as we did in the past." Yet here we were in a building that not even the most radical of loony-lefty, establishment-hating councils would have found fit for purpose.

At least the courtroom itself was as it should have been in terms of elegance and splendour. It was, in fact, a near facsimile of any courtroom in England, and, lack of crown aside, would not have looked out of place in Manchester or Leeds. The judge presiding, topped off by the traditional English wig, was an imposing yet witty Chinese woman who obviously took the ceremony very seriously. Dozens of friends and family choked the courtroom, with many more stuck outside watching proceedings on TV. It all felt rather fun, in a sombre kind of way.

In total there were eight men and women being sworn in: two barristers, including Sid, plus six solicitors. Seven were ethnically Chinese, two of whom were raised in America and one in Shanghai. Although some of their English wasn't the best I had ever heard, the fact that they had passed all their English language exams meant that they must have been superbly qualified. Each of the lawyers was introduced to the judge by their master, which gave them the chance to show off a little about their protégés. Not all of it was especially flattering, like the girl who was described as being a control-freak, and the bloke who was obviously so boring that the master spent more time talking about himself. But overall the families and friends were outwardly satisfied by the speeches, if the level of applause was any way to measure things. The judge finished the ceremony with a short talk—the only part of the morning that was translated into Cantonese—about how important their positions would be from now on, and then they were off into the serious world of the law. I wished Sid good luck, and headed back out into the rain.

TWENTY-TWO

....

One Saturday morning in early March we sat in a restaurant enjoying a breakfast pizza—what a good but unhealthy idea—when a man wearing a crash helmet walked past the window. Two minutes later he returned, strolling in the other direction. He repeated this process a dozen times or so, looking like a geographically confused bank robber, until he finally disappeared. It was an odd thing to watch.

Later that day we were enjoying a cup of tea with some new friends, Nick and Laura, a sickening couple whose ultra-good looks were matched only by their personal warmth and their sense of adventure. Nick, with a rugged blonde appearance and a Terry Thomas smile, had been telling us about some ultra-race he had just run across Cambodia, when, in an effort to change the subject to something that made me feel less lazy, I mentioned crash helmet head.

"Oh, that was Simon," said Laura, not remotely surprised by me bringing this up. "He's my boss. I think he was just looking for something."

"Wouldn't it have been easier for him to look for whatever it was without his helmet on?"

"He doesn't think like that. He is an artist." I wasn't sure if she was mentioning his profession as an excuse or a reason, but whatever the sense it did kick off a conversation about a forthcoming art exhibition that Laura, an event organiser, was arranging for him.

Hong Kong wasn't necessarily known for its art scene, but scratch the surface and there were enough wannabe artists to whet the creative appetite. We had already seen one show, but that bank-sponsored event had been aimed at those wealthy enough to buy a Damien Hirst sculpture on a whim. Which is why when Larry scarpered off into a decidedly expensive installation in the form of a bamboo cage we were surprised that the curator didn't immediately tell him/us off.

"Art is meant to be interacted with," she said, once she had removed her hand from her forehead and ungritted her teeth.

The event that Laura was helping to put on for her employer, as well as other Hong Kong artists, was in a spacious black room in Tai Koo Shing. As well as Nick and Laura, we seemed to know a bunch of other people there too, all there separately and tucking into the copious canapés. This was a bit of a watershed moment for us; seeing a variety of different people we recognised made us, for the first time, feel part of a wider social scene. This was not a common thing to feel in Hong Kong, as a number of folks had told us that their social lives were very disparate, with none of their friends actually knowing each other. This was understandable as pals were often from different sources, such as work, hobbies, friends of friends from home, and so on, unlike in the West where most of someone's social circle tends to come from one main source. This meant that it was possible to feel unconnected to Hong Kong society as a whole, much like solitary dots on a canvas with nothing to link them together. This could be unsettling if you were used to having a gang of mates as we had enjoyed in London. But here, even if the people we knew weren't necessarily aware of the existence of each other, at least they were all showing interest in the same event, which was a start.

With free booze and food it was no surprise to bump into Tom there. I spied him by the champagne bar, chatting up two stunningly attractive Chinese girls and looking like he was having a good time at it.

"Ah, look who it is," said Nick as he pointed to Tom. I wasn't aware that they were friends, so was pleased to see our network expanding.

Soon Tom gave up his chase and came to join us on a tour of the exhibition. It would be fair to describe some of the pieces as 'nouveau Chinese', infusing influences from the West into a solidly Oriental foundation. Many were simply Western, perhaps reflecting, as someone remarked on our tour, that the market was still rooted in European and American concepts of art.

No matter what the origin, there was a bucket of imagination on display. Not all of it was peaceful, as the giant silver sniper rifle with its twirly barrel placed in the mouth of a polished metal figure showed. High up on one of the walls was a stunning picture of the head of a beautiful Chinese woman, which on closer inspection revealed a smudge of blood below the neckline to show that she had been decapitated.

The highlight, at least for us, was the huge red and gold drum set, placed on a wooden scaffold that reached the ceiling. It was highly memorable for its interactivity; punters were encouraged to whack its skins with the provided drumsticks, making a commotion that was even louder than the wagging of drink-spiked tongues. Aggie's sister, who had flown over for a flying visit, took particular delight in smashing the bejeezus out of them.

Nick and Laura took us, along with Tom, to a nearby eatery after we had had our fill of art. Laura spent hours answering questions on the meanings and thoughts behind the different installations, portraits, and sculptures. Although it was fascinating, it all kind of merged into one for the layman after a while, so eventually the conversation moved to an earthier subject, namely rugby. There were, after all, only a few weeks left to the biggest social event of the Hong Kong calendar and men—and a few women—were becoming seriously excited about a week of beer and sport

TWENTY-THREE

....

I knew the Saturday of the Hong Kong Rugby Sevens was going to be a day of headiness five minutes after Tom and I took our seats. It was 8.30 in the morning, and there were already people in trouble. Steep concrete stairs were not such an easy climb for some, especially those over-indulging themselves with two-pint plastic glasses of lager. One fat, balding guy in too-tight shorts, so hammered he could hardly stand, took a hurtle down the steps of the stadium from the very top to the very bottom, rolling like a sunburnt Humpty Dumpty. Five minutes later and another lad was probably a bit startled to find that his vault over the fence around the stairwell led to a twenty foot drop onto a hapless beer-seller. As I heard no ambulance I assumed they weren't too badly injured.

The Sevens takes place every year in the forty thousand seat Hong Kong Stadium, and anyone remotely fun heads straight to the South Stand. For those not familiar with this particular part of the Stadium, it's very much akin to the Western Terrace at Headingly or the Eric Hollies Stand at Edgbaston; comparisons which probably don't do much for the vast majority of people who don't tour the provincial cricket grounds of England. So perhaps it is best to say that this particular end of the Hong Kong Stadium is where compulsory fancy dress meets chronic consumption of beer and the occasional beef pie. It was here that Tom had led me, for better or worse, and we had had to arrive early because by 9am the South Stand was generally full, a reflection on the twin passions of the average Hong Kong expat, namely socialising and rugby.

Football may be the enduring interest of many of the local Chinese, especially as a game to bet on, but to most expats it is rugby that really ignites passion. With eighteen clubs to choose from there is plenty of competition and many highlights to the season. But without doubt the jewel of the rugby year is the Hong Kong Sevens. In fact, some would argue that this is the apex of rugby the world over, although perhaps only from a drinking perspective would this be true.

Such is the enthusiasm for the Sevens that there is even a dinner to launch the six-month countdown to the tournament. Just after we arrived in Hong Kong, Witto, knowing my love of the game, invited me to join his table at the Long Lunch, as it was simply known. Four hundred men, plus about a dozen or so women, sat down to a three-course meal and more speeches from the sponsors and fund-raisers than was healthy. My immediate table neighbours were quite a diverse bunch, with a quiet, slight Liechtenstein banker on one side, and the loudest Englishman since Johnny Rotten on the other. Jim, from London, with black curly hair and a youthful face, was apparently well-known given the amount of people that came over to say hello as the lunch wore on, probably because everyone in the territory could hear him when said anything. His voice was the biological equivalent of a space shuttle launch, so it was fortunate his chat was quite good.

The organisers had been clever enough to bring in two ex-rugby stars to ensure that the heckling didn't get too out of control: Andy Nichol and Richard Hill. Nichol was very funny indeed and basically gave a stand up performance which had the crowd fully amused. Poor Hill had to follow this up, a task not made easier by him being not exactly a comedian. That said, he did make everyone sit up and notice when he revealed that he hadn't gone drinking after winning the Rugby World Cup in Sydney in 2003 because "I had to get my girlfriend to the airport because she had an incredibly early flight to get back to school." Cue a few surprised faces, and the policemen in the audience starting to twitch.

"No, she is a teacher."

"Tell it to the judge!" shouted Jim.

After lunch everyone went upstairs to a bar to watch the All Blacks kick the living crap out of the Japanese team, all while imbibing endless beers. Curiously Nichol and Hill spent a great deal of the match on their own in the corner, left alone by everyone. They were probably talking about how much they disliked former England international Austin Healey, which was the only common theme between their two speeches. I bailed at this point, having a supper to go to that Aggie had recklessly arranged for me.

When we came home from the restaurant, verging on midnight, we happened to go past the hotel where the lunch had been. There was Jim, momentarily silenced, sitting on the steps at a forty five degree angle with a cigarette poking out of the side of his mouth. His shirt front was coloured in red wine, one arm was out of his suit jacket, and, most noticeably, only one of his shoes remained in place. It had definitely been lunch too far for some.

If this was what the Sevens could do six months before the event, then goodness knew what I would face come March. Indeed, for tens of thousands of tourists from every part of the globe the tournament is mainly about the party rather than the rugby. Not surprisingly then, as the roly-poly man and his jumping friend had shown, the carnage tends to start before the rugby has even been mentioned.

Aside from the sport, we were mightily entertained by the fancy dress. With twenty-four nations competing there were representatives from all over the world, even a troop of Rwandan Stormtroopers who whistled, sang and danced the whole day behind us. We spent hours trying to work out what the girls dressed in airmail envelopes and wearing white veils had come dressed as before it clicked—mail-order brides.

A group of French Smurfs appeared in front of us, wearing white pants and tights and some apt headgear, leaving their torsos exposed to the elements apart from blue body paint. This unfortunately didn't block out the UV from the getting-quite-hot sun, so as the day progressed they all turned a nice shade of purple. They spent the rest of the day being slapped on the back by passing Anglos, no doubt encouraged by the tannoy announcement that greeted the arrival of their national team on the pitch.

"Stand up if you hate the French!" Sadly for the Smurfs, hardly a soul was left seated.

Tom and I were dressed in standard Mexican outfits, with ponchos, small guitars, and glorious moustaches. Although there were quite a few Mexicans in the stand, none of them were real and no one had sombreros as large as ours. Three and a half feet of hat took some beating and, given the strength of the sun, that was a good thing.

The beer and pie throwing started just before lunch time. At least, I think it was beer. Given the queues for the men's loos there was a good chance it wasn't—which is why we had seated ourselves way up at the top of the stand and positioned ourselves under the broadest of hat brims. Despite this, I was assured by the Sevens veterans around me that this behaviour was nothing like it used to be. Gone were the days when the beer-sellers, normally acne-riven teenagers, were forcibly crowd-surfed across the stands. Or when the throng decided to make a mountain out of plastic beer pitchers on the try line, which disappointingly the referee said interfered with the game.

The behaviour may have been tamer, but it was still diverting. An Australian bloke had strapped on a pair of fake breasts where the nipples had been replaced by small taps. These were in turn supplied by an apparently inexhaustible supply of Jägermeister, giving him the nickname 'Jäger Boobs'. Needless to say the girls loved it. All afternoon he had beautiful women slurping from his chest, as well as the odd bloke, all trying to avoid his long blonde wig spilling into their mouths as they drank. It wasn't as if he was a muscle-bound hunk—indeed his puffy lips, wide forehead, and craggy brown jowls hardly put him in the same category as Achilles—but the alcoholic chest appendages seemed to be a highly popular attraction.

Towards the end of the day Nick rang. He had meant to join us but had been mysteriously absent all day. We had written him off as not coming, as he had been out till very late indeed the night before at some rugby-themed dinner, but it soon became clear that Nick had been putting his free-drink finding skills to good use by securing some complementary hospitality in a corporate box. After a solid day of eating and drinking he had decided that it was time to call for reinforcements. As the beer—and worse—was still flying around the South Stand we thought it wise to cut our losses, and with one last view of the girls chatting up Jäger Boobs we headed to what we hoped would be a more civilised affair.

Indeed it was. For a start no one was in fancy dress, and although they didn't stop and stare as us Mexicans walked in, they certainly didn't appear overly impressed by our attire. I smeared my fake moustache back on my lip, hoisted my guitar over my shoulder, and removed the edge of my sombrero from the face of a tall ginger woman trying to chat up her boss.

"Nick? He's outside," said a man mopping the wine from his charcoal suit trousers, wine that had spilt thanks to a swoosh from Tom's hat. We thanked him, gave him a fresh napkin, and attempted to squeeze out to the balcony. We got as far as the first row of seats before we had to give up, as there were simply too many corporate twonks to push past. Instead, we stood for a few minutes watching the game—it was the final of the women's competition, which was proving quite a popular draw with the crowd—hoping that from amongst the scrum in front of us Nick would appear. Finally he did, with an empty glass in hand and a steely look in his eye that said he would be drinking for a long, long time.

I only managed a short while in the box. The day had been long, with good beer and memorable costumes, especially the dozens of groups dressed as Kim Jong Il, and all the corporate souls had squeezed the remaining life out of me. I decided to head home before Nick or Tom could whisk me out to Wanchai and even more trouble. Plus, I was about to start my new job.

TWENTY-FOUR

··

March had started in the best possible way, with me being offered full-time, well-paid employment. It had taken a long time, but the 6am phone call from my US-based future boss was a good thing to be woken up for. I sat on my bed rubbing my eyes and pinching myself that I was actually being given the chance to leave the thin ranks of the unemployed. Aggie was probably happier than me; I would be able to waste my own money on frivolous taxi rides, order more than one bottle of wine at dinner, and buy a new pair of jeans every few years, without recourse to her savings. Having a new job was going to be good for both our sanities.

I had three weeks of extended holiday left, and I was not going to have any trouble filling it. As soon as Aggie left for work I sat at the dining room table and started planning.

One of my most pressing desires was to see a bit more of China proper; to discover the real core of a country I still didn't really know. Aside from the interest factor, I also wanted to try out my new found Mandarin skills. New Moon though was far from enthusiastic when I said I was going to head off on my own into the deepest, reddest People's Republic.

"They won't understand English," she pointed out, quite hurtfully and truthfully.

"But I want to try out my Chinese," I declared. She looked at me for a few sharp seconds, then repeated herself.

My linguistic confidence crushed, I spoke to a friend of mine who happened to travel a great deal around China about whether he knew anyone in the People's Republic that could act as a guide. He did, very vaguely indeed, and they lived in Wuhan.

Most Westerners have never heard of this city of ten million people, a population which would have made it the largest city in the EU. It was actually three cities in one (Wuchang, Hankou, and Hanyang, hence the combination Wuhan), and lay at the edge of a large and fertile plain in Central China, on the Yangtze River. This positioning, plus its numerous transport links, meant that in the never-ending comparison with America it is known by some as the 'Chicago of China'. I was pretty sure that there weren't many large inland lakes, mercantile exchanges, or Italian gangsters there, but I had to go and check it out for myself.

I took a bullet train from Guangzhou. This was a modern marvel of China, in that they had managed to build more miles of high-speed train track than anywhere else, and quicker than any other nation could have done it. Admittedly they rushed the process a fair bit, which led to the deaths of over forty people in a horrendous track failure just before my journey, but hey ho, you can't have it all (said the Communist Party). It really was a smooth ride, with friendly stewardesses and perky fellow passengers who chatted and laughed together. I spent the four hour ride looking out of the window at a near thousand miles of continuous human settlement, sprouting from the semi-tropical trees in the south to the rice paddies further up the line. Blocky grey houses appeared singly or in clumps every few seconds for the entire length of the thousand kilometre journey, a reminder of just how many people lived in China.

The first thing I noticed when we slid into Wuhan was that it wasn't just the railways that were being built. I had been told that there were five thousand construction sites in this city alone, and you could see this was no exaggeration. There was so much dust in the air that I could have bottled it and sold it as aggregate.

Once I had arrived at my hotel—a swanky Western establishment because I didn't feel quite ready for total local immersion just yet—I called Peter, my local contact. I agreed to meet him in the reception at five, but half an hour later he called to say that another modern marvel of China, the enormous expansion of car ownership, was severely delaying him. I settled down to wait by the window with a cup of jasmine tea and a never-ending supply of passers-by to watch.

I was always amazed by the amount of times that Chinese friends, acquaintances, and complete strangers would let me know that all gweilos looked the same. There was absolutely no embarrassment to it either, rather just an accepted fact. This was unlike back in the UK, where a friend was once taken to task for not being able to tell the difference between Japanese and Chinese women, even though a) he'd never been to either country, and b) not even my Japanese friend who is married to a Chinese woman and has spent a decade living in Shanghai can always tell the difference. But I admit that I was a bit puzzled as to how Europeans could be mistaken when they had different colour hair. New Moon was again on hand to explain.

"We Chinese have spent five thousand years looking at faces to tell the difference because all of our hair is black. So what use is there at looking at the top of a person's head? This is why when we look at Westerners we only look at their faces, and all your faces look the same." Well that was that.

One mistake that Hong Kong Chinese never made was in identifying a Mainlander. It would be fair to say that there was no love lost between the two, with those north of the border complaining of their neighbours being 'British lackeys' or 'Running dogs', quite openly and even in print. For their part, Hong Kongers dismissed Mainlanders as 'rude', 'ignorant', and 'filthy' to choose three of the less offensive adjectives I had heard used.

That there was a division in overall Chinese culture—and we haven't even touched on the often intense rivalries between the different Chinese provinces, let alone with Taiwan—would have severely annoyed those dyed-in-the-wool communists who seriously believed that all Chinese folk should look the same. The reason is a fear of the country fragmenting. There is an old Chinese saying which goes "The Empire, once divided, will unite; the Empire, once united, will divide." Ever since Qin Shi Huang became, in 221 BC, the First Emperor of a united China, the country had broken up and reunited more times than Richard Burton and Elizabeth Taylor. It may well be that in a few hundred years scholars will look back at the current nation, held under control of the Communist Party, as being in a periodic state of unification ahead of another nasty split. Time will certainly tell. But the communists were taking no chances, and invested plenty of energy into ensuring that China's inhabitants all felt thoroughly and homogeneously Chinese. One day I took the ferry up the river to see a friend of mine called Alan who ran a factory in a small, anonymous Pearl River Delta town called Daliang. This would be the thirteenth largest settlement in the UK, such is the scale of China. He took me to lunch with his factory manager, Xi, who dismissed my comment that there seemed to be a great deal of diversity in the looks of people from different corners of the country.

"All Chinese look the same, from north or south, east or west. We all have black hair and our faces are very similar." He then stared at me with an intensity that really made me feel quite uncomfortable and unwilling to challenge him. Luckily the meal, including my first taste of chilli jellyfish, was a surprisingly delicious distraction, so we were able to continue without any recourse to my comment. But I would have liked to have said something to Xi because even to a blind man Chinese faces had huge variation. High cheekbones indicated a northern origin, whereas darker skin on a small, wiry frame told of a southern lineage. Xi though was having none of it. For him, genetics was surpassed by politics, and nothing was going to change his mind or that of the Party. The survival of China depended on it, apparently.

Hong Kongers could tell Mainlanders not just from their faces. There was actually more variation in terms of dress, manners, and attitudes, some subtle and some as obvious as a pink penguin in a polar bear enclosure. Waiting in line at Ocean Park made you acutely aware of the differences between locals and those from across the border. Whereas a Kowloon native is happy to queue patiently, British-style, those residents of Guangzhou, Shenzhen, or anywhere up north barged past with a determination that would make a German tourist blush. I asked a taxi driver about this once, and he advised me to extend my arms and shout to stop them from pouring past you. Whilst my English reserve didn't really permit me to go this far and give the queue-bargers a verbal lashing, I did find that extending my arms rapidly and unexpectedly was a useful tool in preventing unwanted overtaking.

I remembered a sign on the Star Ferry on my first visit to Hong Kong that said 'No spitting'. Graham and I looked at each other and laughed, thinking someone had put it up for a joke. Indeed, hawking up in Hong Kong was a pretty rare sight, but on the Mainland projecting spittle with force appeared to be a national habit. On the way from Wuhan train station to my hotel my driver averaged a spit a minute, carefully winding down his window just enough to be able to fire the green mess into the street without letting too much of the street dust in to fill his cab. After the fifth time I thought it prudent to shift over just in case his aim failed.

Assuming that the Mainlanders weren't pushing in or using the pavement as an unfillable spittoon, how else would you tell them apart from Hong Kongers? As I sat watching the people of Wuhan traipse past the window I realised that if Harry Enfield was writing his sketch shows in modern day Hong Kong the Scousers would be from across the border. It looked like the majority of the country had been taking fashion tips from pictures of Liverpool circa 1989; never had so much nylon been on show. Shell suits were the choice of the majority, and everyone else seemed to be in ill-fitting grey trousers and dirty 'white' man-made fibre shirts that first started life in a North Sea oil well. When I compared this with the high fashion of Hong Kong, the contrast was distinct to say the least.

TWENTY-FIVE

....

I was pondering Chinese fashion sense when Peter finally arrived. He may have been the friend of a friend of a friend but he greeted me with the warmth of a long lost cousin. Dressed in natural fibres and speaking good English, he was quite different to the other inhabitants of the city, partly because he wasn't actually from Wuhan. After our initial introduction he asked me if I was hungry. Yes, I was, so we stepped out of the hotel and towards the river for a bite to eat. We entered a Sichuan 'hotpot' restaurant and took a table in the corner, surrounded by small groups of men and women in their twenties dressed invariably in black and white nylon.

We were met at the entrance by a plump, sweaty Chinese girl dressed contrarily in brown nylon, who actually looked Burmese and therefore about as similar to a Shanghainese woman as I did—an observation that would no doubt have seriously annoyed Xi. She took us over to sit at what appeared to be a mini-volcano. The centre of the table was taken up by a round metal cauldron, around two feet across, sunken into the body of the wood, and filled with a liquid that resembled peppercorns floating in gurgling blood. It turned out I was half right. It was pepper, but it was actually suspended in boiling chilli oil. In the middle of this gastronomic inferno was another, smaller soup-bowl-sized dish that was filled with what appeared to be milk, but which was probably something equally spicy. Back in Britain I had been renowned for my love of all things hot, but this was surely above and beyond even the most sordid of student union hot sauce eating contests.

Peter received a tray full of raw beef from the waitress and slid the contents into the red froth; the resultant bubbling looked like a shark feeding frenzy. After a few minutes of staring he instructed to me to take out some of the by-now cooked meat, which I gingerly ate.

It felt like my mouth had been run over, beaten, then placed in a Mexican narco's acid bath. I thought my lips and tongue were going to fall off. Peter grinned at my shock, picked up his bottle of beer, chinked mine, and tucked into his own plate.

After about ten seconds of sheer sensory terror something odd happened: I wanted more. I had discovered, after about a billion people before me, a new drug. I popped some beef into my mouth, which this time felt like it was merely clipped by a passing car and given a light slap. The next bite was less painful still, and in no time I had managed to limit my suffering to a mere dig in the ribs each time. But like an old beaten-up drunk I wanted more. Plate after plate was consumed, the conversation shelved while I enjoyed my newfound addiction in relative peace.

We finished the night off with a walk along the main street next to the Yangtze, which was scattered with old colonial buildings left over from when the city of Hankou was a British-dominated open port. Many of these grey stone monuments to past Western power were abandoned, but some were occupied by the occasional bar and restaurant, taking advantage of their position overlooking the river. It was to the river that we next headed, for a ferry ride across its wide expanse. We sat in the open air, surrounded by giggling teenagers and old grandmothers, plus the odd scooter, feeling the engines strain under the pressure of the current as we made the mile-long trip back and forth. It felt momentous to be atop one of the greatest rivers in the world, somewhere that I had only ever thought about in the abstract. Now I was sailing on it, and it really did feel like a large tick on the bucket list.

The next day, slightly hungover and with severe internal burning, I headed out with Peter to do the rounds of Wuhan. First on our list was the Yellow Crane Tower, a sort of super-pagoda that stands on a hill overlooking the city and is, so I understood, famous in China for being 'the first tower under heaven.' Peter was more interested in the Japanese tour group that was there, its elderly members dressed in baseball caps and no nylon.

"What are they doing here?" he whispered, in a not overly friendly manner.

All towered out, we went to a street market for an early lunch. It was located in a pedestrianised alley, where the stalls and restaurants were advertised by neon signs set into the grey walls, and run by women wearing medical face masks and red, white, and even tartan nylon. They served hungry punters by the hundred from huge ceramic bowls that they constantly stirred and re-filled.

It was in the back of one of these eating establishments, seated on a yellow plastic chair, that I was fortunate enough to be introduced to 'chou tofu' (literally 'stinky tofu'). I'd like to say it was nice, but it actually smelt and tasted like horse-sweat-tinged manure. Peter grinned through his thick glasses and asked, after I had struggled gamely through three quarters of the serving, if I was still hungry.

"Not so much, actually." But by then it was too late; he had ordered another local specialty, 'ri gan mian'—hot dry noodles with a sesame flavour, covered by some sort of black lumpy sauce that didn't taste too bad at all. I chewed some down, but before I could finish even more arrived, in the form of rubbery skewered chilli squid, and an orange, melon, and tomato salad covered in red bean sauce. Peter hoovered up his four courses at speed, and was soon looking bored as I waded through, one noodle or bean at a time. I thought I would give him something to talk about by asking him about the Japanese we had seen. His face immediately changed to be intensely serious, his brow furrowed and his eyes cold.

"They did many bad things to my country," he began. "Those Japanese people we saw, they were old, they may have been in the war. They all knew they were killing many Chinese, many British and other people too. But they pretend it never happened. They never say sorry properly. They lie and say that we exaggerate." He was, by this stage, quite animated. After a ten second pause, he finished with a statement of real intent: "One day we will make them say sorry." Although I was quite aware of the Japanese record in Asia—millions and millions were murdered, sometimes in the most brutal ways imaginable—it was intriguing to see the bitterness still so alive, for example in comparison with European attitudes to modern-day Germany. I didn't ask, but I was willing to bet he didn't drive a Toyota.

It was time to depoliticise the day and so we headed to the Hubei Provincial Museum. The highlight was without doubt artefacts belonging to the old Marquis Yi of Zeng, an aristocrat that lived in the region in the fifth century BC. His tomb—made in four parts to represent a palace of his day and accidentally discovered by the People's Liberation Army in 1977 when they were 'trying to destroy a hill'—has one of the largest collections of ritual bronze pieces ever discovered. The highlight was the large, sixty-five-strong set of two-tone bells (hit one side and it chimes one note; strike the other side and a different note sounds) and accompanying instruments. These were periodically used to recreate ancient music to apparent critical acclaim, according to the museum. A beautiful metal crane, complete with deer antlers and a neck to make even the tallest giraffe jealous, was my personal favourite, although the bronze cast of the head of the Marquis himself, with a fat nose, bald head, and chubby cheeks, was quite remarkable too.

One not-so-nice exhibit was the list of women buried with the Marquis upon his death in 433 BC. I took a guess that all these women didn't coincidentally drop dead at the same time as their husband/lover/master so one could only imagine their reaction as they realised that the Marquis had reached the end of his life: "Uh-oh" was probably quick to their lips.

It would have been a good time to leave town, although I suppose there was always the possibility that these were volunteers. Whatever the reason for their presence here, they were all young, ranging from thirteen to twenty-six, and incredibly small, with an average height of just five feet. Some were buried with stringed instruments, some with beads, some with not much at all. But all were now immortalised, albeit in a functional museum under communist rule, which was probably not quite what they would have had in mind for the afterlife.

I would have liked to have stayed longer in Wuhan. I had only been there for a few days and there was an awful lot more to see, plus a great deal of conversation to have with Peter. He really was quite an interesting man, with knowledge about all the different parts of the city we went through and a thorough understanding of China's role in the modern world. It turned out that we had two things in common. First was a fondness for music, which I discovered when he took me to the Brussels Bar to watch a live set by a quite stunning female singer, whose voice was one of the best I had heard in a lifetime of gig-going. The second was that we were both about to start new jobs. His was in a town near Shanghai, as an engineer in a car company. Mine was back in Hong Kong, and with only a couple of days left before I was due at my desk, I headed home. I had waited long enough for the right job to come along to not screw it up by failing to turn up on day one.

TWENTY-SIX

....

A couple of hundred years before the Marquis of Zeng was popping his clogs, in 636 BC to be precise, another minor Chinese aristocrat was wandering around the countryside trying to avoid being killed by his brother, a duke, in the way that some families do. As legend has it, one day he and his entourage stopped for a rest. Given that the group had no food, Chong'er, the aristo concerned, was probably a touch surprised to be given a bowl of steaming meat soup. However it's pretty certain that this level of surprise was surpassed when, upon enquiring whence the flesh for the meal had appeared, his old friend Jie chirpily remarked that he had cut it from his own thigh.

Many of us might struggle to show our gratitude for this act of self-harm and unintended cannibalism, but not Chong'er. He remembered the sacrifice for the rest of his life. Jie though was not one to be praised, and when Chong'er eventually took over from his brother and became Duke, he fled into a forest. Chong'er was determined to reward Jie, so went to look for him. After searching through the trees for a while he was about to give up when his advisers came up with the most cunning plan; set fire to the woods to flush him out. Unfortunately, this piece of inspired advice had the adverse effect of killing poor Jie. So remorseful was his old friend and master that he banned the heating of food for three days in memory of thigh-meat Jie. And that, apparently, is how the April festival of Qing Ming started.

Given that Qing Ming was now about the reverence of one's ancestors, played out by visiting their graves and sweeping them clean, it was anyone's guess as to how Jie's leg meat became its inspiration. I asked New Moon about this and, although she remembered her grandmother telling her something about this when she was young, that was about as much as she could add, and not a single one of my colleagues could elucidate further. This is one of the remarkable things about Chinese culture; when you have five thousand years of tradition to call upon, you aren't going to remember how it all fits together.

Tom and I pondered this as we enjoyed a beer at a packed pub in Soho. We could tell it was a holiday eve because every expat in Hong Kong was drinking ahead of a welcome lie-in the next day. As Hong Kong seemed to have more mid-week public holidays than anywhere else, on account of the mix of Western and Chinese festivals, there were plenty of excuses for non-weekend parties.

Not wanting to ignore the festival completely, Tom and I spent a while looking up the meaning of Qing Ming on our phones, but after a while were interrupted by a young Anglo-Chinese man sitting next to us at the bar who had overheard our conversation. Henry, with small, fat-encircled eyes and a mouth like a puckered apple, was certainly knowledgeable about Qing Ming, and had no hesitation in explaining it all.

"Most families go to the graves of their parents or grandparents, give them a quick clean, and leave some flowers. But if you're really Chinese, especially Daoist, you do things a bit differently, because they believe in giving them stuff to enjoy in the afterlife."

These offerings were, so we were told, normally in the form of food, tea, joss sticks, wine, and chopsticks.

"Others," continued Henry between gulps of his beer, "prefer to buy them a few luxuries. Some even take cut-out paper images of all the things that they need where they're gone, like cars, or helpers."

"Helpers? You mean, like Filipina helpers?"

"Yep. They like make a paper doll, colour it in, and take it to the cemetery. Then they burn it. Which is a bit weird because you'd think the ancestors wouldn't want a burnt helper, but there you go."

Paper helpers aside, there are plenty of shops that stock all the grave goods that a deceased Daoist could want. This may look a tad strange in the eyes of a Westerner, and indeed not all Hong Kongers think it rational, but at least people are making a personal effort. This is in direct contrast to others, especially on the Mainland, who can't be bothered to do anything themselves and so pay fake mourners to weep and wail at their parent's final resting place. What a good inspiration for children everywhere.

I awoke the next day with my brain addled but at least knowing a lot more about the festival we were celebrating. Not having any nearby graves to visit we decided to head out to the New Territories again.

This time we headed to Sai Kung, a town in the north-east of Hong Kong about an hour from our flat. Compared to London or New York, being able to escape the environs of the city was a quick journey. But it wasn't half convoluted: a taxi to Central, followed by the MTR to Hang Hau station in Kowloon; then a long queue for a minibus which never came, forcing us to instead take a taxi to Sai Kung.

Once we arrived we began to wonder whether the effort had been worth it. For many expats, Sai Kung resonated as a small country town which people moved to once they were jaded with the urban life of Hong Kong Island.

"It's ever so nice in Sai Kung," was a phrase often heard in the pub. Well, it really depended on your experience, I suppose. If you'd lived in a forty-four-storey tower block your whole life then Sai Kung may have appeared to be the bucolic idyll that many painted it to be. If, however, you had grown up amongst the wheat fields of England then it was more like a Chinese version of Felixstowe.

The Sai Kung streets were the normal Hong Kong scene, just on a smaller scale: cut price clothes retailers, seafood restaurants with overcrowded tanks of soon-to-be-fried fish, and hardware stores with more stock than the entire industrial output of Tanzania. A few expat pubs, inhabited by bald middle-aged men playing pool and comparing tattoos, were sprinkled around the minute town centre. The waterfront, or promenade, was memorable, but only for being choked by pleasure-craft seeking to take the thousands of Mainland tourists out on island cruises. One boat specialised in taking students wishing to "understand nature and write projects and presentations"—not something you'd see often in Lowestoft or Folkestone for sure. We resisted the temptation for water-borne entertainment and instead stopped drink at a small café. Here we made the digestive mistake of ordering local coffee, which had the look and taste of dark, bitter cement. Rather disappointed with the whole Sai Kung experience, we jumped into another taxi and headed further north into the real countryside.

The Sai Kung Country Park is a hilly wilderness, crossed by several concreted trails and covered by deep woods. Our taxi took us along a narrow, dusty track, squeezing past buses and cars and avoiding the occasional road-walker, before dropping us at what looked like a Victorian bandstand. This landmark, the sign stated, somewhat incongruously marked the start of a paved path heading to the coast. Larry was quite happy walking for a few minutes at a time, particularly when he could sprint off on the downhill sections, so my shoulders got a bit more of a rest than I was expecting. Aggie meanwhile was packed to the gunnels with waterproofs, hats, sunscreen, spare t-shirts, food, and several mega bottles of water, testament to the fact that the weather didn't seem to know if it was winter, spring, or early summer. We threaded through the trees, stopping occasionally for a swig of water and a chance to look over the reservoir that ran to our right.

The woodland in Hong Kong can be quite thick, so many a trail has been cut through the trees to stop repetitions of Chong'er and Jie's disastrous wandering. Before 1841 Hong Kong had been stripped of its forestry by centuries of visiting firewood collectors, but now, thanks to the application of an early governor who had decided to replant the colony, there are trees everywhere. Given that the area straddles the zone between tropical and temperate, there is much higher biodiversity than would be expected for a territory of its size, particularly in terms of vegetation. There are three thousand varieties of flowering plants including one hundred and twenty orchids and over three hundred native tree species, as well as numerous foreign interlopers. In comparison the UK has around fifty indigenous types of orchid, and only thirty-three native tree varieties, in an area two hundred times the size. It is a botanist's paradise.

After an hour or so wandering through the trees, we reached the seaside village of Sai Wan. The beach was really quite enticing, with big waves, sweeping open sand, and perhaps more reminiscent of somewhere in the UK than in Hong Kong. Larry played for a while in the waves, refusing to pose nicely for some Mainland tourists who eventually cried out "How can we trap him for our photo?" much to our annoyance. We had lunch at the beach-front restaurant, ordering a full round of fried rice and fresh coconut milk. We had heard that it may have been possible to take a speedboat from another beach nearby straight back to Sai Kung, but after seeking the advice of some keen looking hikers who had even more kit than us, we decided this wasn't the best idea as apparently the boat sometimes never turns up. The thought of fruitlessly waiting for hours wasn't especially appetising, and even less so with the weather so changeable. We trudged back to the pavilion, where we caught a bus back to the disappointing Sai Kung, and then home. Still, being the country folk we are, it felt good to be back amongst the trees and the woods again, although there were perhaps less sheep and wheat than our childhood selves would have been used to.

TWENTY-SEVEN

....

A few months earlier my friend Alistair had asked if he and his wife Amelia could come over for Easter. At the time I hadn't been working and so this seemed like a good idea, but now I was a couple of weeks into my new job. I was nonetheless determined to show them a good time, which called for drastic action: a trip to Macau.

This former Portuguese colony, which was originally settled by Iberian traders in the sixteenth century, had long held an infamous reputation for gambling, partying, and prostitutes. It sounded like the perfect place to entertain visitors.

When I first came to this colonial cousin of Hong Kong in 1996 the main casino in town was the Lisboa, owned by one of the most extraordinary men in modern Chinese history. Stanley Ho, it was fair to say, was not someone to hide his enormously wealthy, influential, and some would say ill-gotten light under any bushel. The ninth of thirteen children from a wealthy Hong Kong family, he fled to neutral Macau when the Japanese invaded. There he quickly built up a fortune based, according to the gossip and allegations, on a thorough disregard for the word 'collaboration', providing Japanese forces with goods hard to find elsewhere. It was also alleged that he made another fortune arming the Communist forces during the Korean War. His real masterstroke though was in winning the Macau casino monopoly, which helped him gather a nest egg of around $3 billion.

Sadly for Stanley, the monopoly was broken by the Macau government in 2002, three years after China regained sovereignty. Some say that this was because not enough money was offered in bribes, but it's hard to tell what really happened given the opacity of the place. What was for sure is that Stanley didn't suffer too much. He still retained half of the registered casinos there, and even owned the ferries that took Hong Kong's addicted gamblers on the short trip across the sea.

What was different now was the fact that Ho was not the only brand name in town anymore. Many of the Las Vegas operations had moved in, or were at least planning to, and of these the biggest and brashest was the Venetian. With a surfeit of fake gold trim and gaudy frescoes, bathed in realistic artificial light to prevent the onset of tiredness in its gamblers, it was even more vulgar than the solid gold toilet that was rumoured to have at one time existed in Hong Kong, and offered pretty similar symbolism.

With so much spent on a tacky interior, it was good for them that they were making money. According to one of the staff, the Macau site generated more revenue in a month than the Vegas version did in a whole year. Once inside it was not hard to see why. The cigarette-smoke-filled expanse, as large as a light aircraft hangar, was filled with Chinese punters hunched over hundreds of card tables and one-armed bandits. In America it was customary to give out free alcohol to gamblers to make them lose their inhibitions. In Macau, not only was there no need to encourage them, but the booze would only have got in the way of slipping some more coins into the slot. It was a truly awesome display of focus.

After dropping our bags at the hotel, we headed back out into the streets to find Fernando's, a restaurant of the highest gastronomic fame. Regulars to Macau took the free casino shuttle buses everywhere, but we were newcomers so took taxis instead. This was one of the main differences to Hong Kong, in that the journey was more than a couple of pounds and we had to wait for about ten minutes to get one. Still, it was more tolerable than the most noticeable difference: immigration. We had queued for about an hour once we disembarked from the ferry, standing in line behind dozens of Mainland Chinese who were treated with the same suspicion and disdain that Arabs are at many Western airports. When it came to our turn at the passport check it became obvious that, while the officials might not have been under the control of the Portuguese authorities any more, they still retained their cultural influence. The man inspecting me lounged back on his chair in a manner of someone waking up from a long siesta, chatting with his colleagues, and clearly wishing he was back in bed. Hong Kong immigration officials on the other hand, while not as nattily dressed, at least made an effort to be as efficient as possible and didn't sit gossiping with each other.

Anyway, back to Fernando's. The restaurant was located on one side of a garden that was home to a couple of hairy dogs, a washing line, and a circular bar made of wood. We chalked our name on the do-it-yourself waiting list which indicated that we had a good few hours to kill before we could eat, so the rest of the gang relaxed at an outside table while I went to the bar to order.

I immediately saw that this was not going to be a quick process, given that there were twenty people waiting but precisely no one to serve them. After about five minutes a frazzled young Filipina arrived carrying a bowl of bread and cheese, opened a couple of bottles of beer, and handed the whole lot to a chino-wearing man who was quite clearly running short of patience. Back home, whether in England or Hong Kong, I would have been the first person to insist on good manner at the bar, not pushing in and smiling graciously if someone was served ahead of the queue. In Fernando's this kind of behaviour wasn't remotely on the cards. Happily the barmaid randomly chose me next, and I grabbed the chance quicker than Lindsay Lohan in an off-licence. It was time to stock up as we had a long wait ahead till lunch.

Three hours and many drinks later we were shown to our table, with a red and white check cover and squished in between a colourful mix of old, young, white, and Chinese, with words in Portuguese, Cantonese, and English flitting around us. The meal was delicious, a medley of Macao rice, chilli prawns, chicken and steak, washed down by Fanta-full sangria, a sign that a bit of Portugal really does survive in the East. Our post-food walk along the beach proved this even more, as we encountered battered old playgrounds littering the promenade shaded by distinctly Mediterranean-themed trees. It was much more Lisbon than Hong Kong.

Back at the Venetian, we rested a while in our apartment-sized rooms before meeting in the bar downstairs. This was where the cultural difference between the West and China became strikingly noticeable. Whilst the gambling floors were totally full of Chinese, there were approximately only four of them in the voluminous bar. Virtually all of its clientele were white or Indian, chugging cocktails and wine on a Biblical scale. We thought the arrival of the American tribute band, led by a singer passing with more than a striking resemblance to a living Whitney Houston on a drug-free day, would summon a few more Chinese, but no. Blackjack and craps still held the premier allure.

The only hint we were in China was the half-time entertainment, which was a flock of local girls who came on stage in next to nothing, wiggled around in time to hard-techno music, and finished their act with even less clothes on. Our wives responded by calling over one of the waitresses to ask where the male totty was; the girl replied that she had been asking for Chippendale types for years without success.

Come 2am and Aggie, who even before she was married with children liked to be tucked up in bed before 11pm, was still going strong. It clicked that this was because of the oxygen that was being pumped into the air, which had the added benefit of diluting the reeking smell of stale Mainland tobacco. The fresh air was keeping more than the customers alert. Several South-East Asian prostitutes, dressed in 1970s faded bling, had taken up position between the bar and the men's loos, forlornly propositioning me and Al as we went to and fro. Naturally enough, the wives were not too chuffed with this. Eventually we all decided enough was enough, so the wives went looking for the twenty-four hour bakery while Al and I went over to the craps table. We found a bunch of Brits there, all uproariously drunk and having a loud time to the bemusement of the serious Chinese gamblers. They were just about tolerated until one of the men, unsteady of hand and foot, threw the dice so hard that they flew off ten feet down the hall. A croupier had a word and we were soon the only non-Chinese on the table. We in turn only lasted an hour until we were broke, and so tired that even the extra oxygen lost its rejuvenating power.

The next day we had a greasy buffet breakfast—the Venetian really didn't like to give out anything of quality for free—then headed back through the lackadaisical immigration and home to Hong Kong.

Al and I had to go to Kowloon to pick up Larry. Tessie had kindly agreed to look after him for the three days we were away, but as it was Easter Sunday she had taken him to the church that she went to every Sunday.

Our experience with churches in Hong Kong had, up to this point, been restricted to vanilla Anglican. On one of our first Sundays we had taken advantage of being woken up early by a screaming child to head to St John's Cathedral, down in Central. The Church of England has a canny ability to place itself at the centre of political life in many countries, and Hong Kong is a prime example. St John's lay right at the heart of the government district, and as such it was notable that the Cathedral was the only freehold land in the whole of Hong Kong.

St John's may not have been to the same scale as a British cathedral, but it certainly, at least to a layman's eye, resembled a thirteenth-century English church. Its whitewashed walls sat in a simple square surrounded by enormous skyscrapers and the few remaining colonial government buildings. A cross commemorating both World Wars had been placed at the centre of its small lawn, alongside the grave of a certain Private Ronald Douglas Maxwell (1919 – December 23, 1941), who was killed in the Battle of Hong Kong and hastily buried there. After the war permission was granted to leave his grave undisturbed, so he remained the only person laid to rest in the Cathedral grounds.

What St John's lacked in size it made up for in numbers. We arrived as the 8am service was finishing, just in time to see a packed congregation take its leave. Oh well, we thought, they must do church earlier than in the UK. But no: our service started semi-busy, but people kept arriving all the way through, until after about forty minutes there was standing room only. There must have been four hundred and fifty people there, easily—and remember that this is just one of six Sunday services—and the curious thing was, four hundred of them were Filipinas. Being the traditional day off for the maids, most of them seem to use their Sundays to go to church. As the vast majority of Filipinas were followers of Rome, it could only be imagined how many of them were at the Catholic establishments.

There were a few things different about the Anglican service here. First was that the hymns were sung quietly, perhaps because many of those at the service didn't have English as a first language and Tell Out My Soul didn't so easily trip off a Tagalog tongue. Second, the congregation was asked to pray for the "President of the People's Republic and the Chief Executive of Hong Kong" rather than the Queen, which showed remarkable political deftness. Third, at the sign of the peace, the congregation didn't shake hands, but merely looked at each other and nodded. This of course was a mysophobic hangover from the horrors of SARS, so what I did at communion caused a little panic.

With four hundred and fifty people to get through, there were numerous little communion stations dotted around the altar, each with a limbering queue of Filipinas and the odd Westerner, including the statutory Englishman wearing Bermuda shorts, black ankle socks, black brogues, and an untucked work shirt. I was given the bread with no problems, but to my embarrassment it was only at the moment of popping the wafer into my mouth that I noticed the girl in front dipping her bread into the wine chalice, rather than sipping out of it. I briefly toyed with disgorging the by-this-stage soggy flake, but thought this might not be the done thing either. All I could manage was "Oh, you do things differently here." To my relief, and the horror of the hundred people behind me in the queue, the priest took a quick look at me and announced "Don't worry, you can drink." A hundred searing eyes told me that I had better learn this difference for next time.

It was with ceremonies in mind that we headed to our first Chinese wedding. This is one heck of an industry, especially when you consider how picky most Chinese women are and that it's a miracle anyone gets hitched in the first place. The average couple spends around US$29,000 on the whole affair, paying for the lavish banquets, fine clothing, and even dowries that some families still insist on. It was also a magnet for the cultural obsession with numerology.

Whereas in the West the association of numbers with luck or ill-luck is mostly restricted to 'three' and 'seven' on the good side and 'thirteen' and '666' on the bad, in China there is a whole swathe of figures with extra meanings. 'Four' sounds like death so is unsurprisingly unlucky, whereas 'nine' is a number traditionally associated with the Emperor as it signifies 'long-lasting.' Dowries, when paid, are therefore generally full of nines. 'Eight' is a very lucky number, sounding as it does like the word for wealth. As such, days with an eight in the date are the most fortuitous to choose for a wedding: 8/8/08, apart from being the start of the Beijing Olympics, was also a bumper time for nuptials. And of course, this being China, there are plenty of fortune tellers to recommend, at a high price, which day with an eight in it is best for your own wedding.

Photos are also a huge part of the nuptials. Most couples seem to spend a whole day having photos taken before the wedding itself. There were even huge studios in Kowloon and the New Territories, specifically dedicated to the task of photographing the bride and groom in as many different styles and costumes as possible. A colleague told me that she and her fiancé spent eight hours on their shoot, without time to even eat, which she considered so unremarkable in comparison with her friends that she was puzzled as to why I thought it excessive. Sometimes we would see the photos being taken outdoors, especially up at Victoria Peak Gardens. One particularly memorable shoot involved a couple in a series of costumes that really didn't fit their portly frames. Having started with smart suits, they then switched to Liverpool Football Club strips, which in turn were replaced by a Superman and Superwoman ensemble, followed by Dastardly and Muttley foam-filled outfits, and finally, to wrap it all up with a summer theme, beach wear. These five changes took over two hours, which would probably have been quicker if they hadn't had to get changed under a public tree, holding up a towel to protect their modesty.

Given that the average monthly household income is only $2,800 it's no surprise that some couples get married in McDonalds. Not Michael and Jenny though, friends from Aggie's work. They were only having a small do, but had decided to have it at the exclusive W hotel over on Kowloon. We really didn't know what to expect, but were looking forward to a new experience. Which, at first, it wasn't. The civil ceremony was in English and almost exactly the same as any we had attended back in London, even down to the accompanying tunes, played on a synthesiser by a bespectacled youth in an ill-fitting suit. He seemed to be having a great time, closing his eyes and only lifting his fingers from the keyboard to sweep back a greasy tuft of hair that would occasionally fall over his lenses. The rest of the guests, mainly from an extended Chinese family liberally scattered around the world, were decidedly unanimated as they waited for the bride to appear, but that was probably because they were all jet-lagged.

What made the whole affair different to its English equivalent was the banquet that followed. With food being so central to Hong Kong culture, the feast was always going to be extravagant. Traditionally the banquet is kicked off by the guests handing over red envelopes, each containing cash for the new couple, before everyone sits down to enjoy a good feed. We duly handed over our envelope to a woman at the front desk who ticked us off her 'contribution list', and we headed to our table to get stuck into the food. Happily for our bellies, Michael and Jenny provided a generous number of courses including one of exquisite barbeque pork, one of poached chicken, then a lettuce-type dish, and also a bowl of soup that I really hoped didn't have any shark fin in it. Then there was something that was completely new.

"What's that?" I asked my neighbour, a glamorous Australian relative of the groom who had been born in Hong Kong but moved to Sydney to study and work.

"Oh, it's delicious. Haven't you had abalone and sea cucumber before?" No I hadn't, and I soon realised why. Whilst I didn't really warm to the abalone, it wasn't even in the same league as its plate-mate. The Wikipedia entry for sea cucumbers says it all as a food item: "They are marine animals with a leathery skin and an elongated body containing a single, branched gonad. Sea cucumbers are found on the sea floor worldwide." Chinese tradition says it is an aphrodisiac, so perfect for a wedding feast in theory, although I wasn't convinced that eating an animal that has the distinctive habit of regurgitating its own intestines would put me in the mood. Still it was a wedding so I ate it not to appear rude. Mind you, not everyone at Chinese weddings felt the need to be polite, such as the oft repeated story of the Mainland couple who used a bank teller machine to check the cash gifts for fakes.

Another obvious difference from a Western wedding was the lack of booze. That wasn't to say that people weren't drinking, but it was very much a one-glass event for most as the food was washed down with tea, like any other local meal. My Aussie neighbour smiled and looked relived when I pointed out this difference, recalling the last marriage she had been to in Sydney which had ended in a brawl between uncle and nephew over a girl they both fancied. I conceded that bucketfuls of beer and wine did add an element of unpredictability to the event, but on the positive side it normally meant there was more gossip in the morning. Funnily enough, as someone that didn't imbibe, she didn't think this was a great trade-off.

The focus on food and not drink meant that the banquet ended with a whimper, as people finished their last course—fried rice—and just stood up and left. We stuck around at the end, hoovering up the last of the wine from our table and finally having a chance to talk to the sober and knackered husband and wife.

"It's probably a bit different to your wedding," said Jenny, and we agreed. How right she was; by this time in the evening we hadn't even finished the speeches, and the band was still just warming up. And there was certainly less gonad representation on the menu.

....

TWENTY-EIGHT

T he lack of alcohol was, in the end, no bad thing as we were up early the next day to head out exploring again. We had decided to go for a stroll around Pokfulam, situated at the western end of Hong Kong Island and somewhere that was described by many, rather optimistically, as a place of rural solitude. That said, the taxi drive along Victoria Road (or, to be more precise, Victoria Jubilee Road, as it was opened in the Empress' Diamond Jubilee year of 1897), felt like a drive along a wild, rocky shore in Europe, totally different to elsewhere on the island. We didn't see a single other car, but did spot dozens of tankers and cargo ships ploughing up and down the coast. Soon though the concrete high-rises of Pokfulam heaved into view and we were brought back to urban reality, although with a pinch we could picture the area as it would have been in the rustic old days.

Then the area was best-known for three things. First was as a water stop for passing ships, who would fill their barrels from what was, in English, known picturesquely as 'Waterfall Creek' and in Cantonese by the somewhat less appealing 'Horse Urine Stream.'

Second, it was the seat of many a fine house built by rich merchants for their weekend getaways. Whilst some wealthy folk were building their homes and holiday houses on the Peak, others were buying up plots of land in Pokfulam to be close to the fresh sea breeze. Perhaps the grandest, and most out of place, of these was a Gothic baronial hall built in the

1860s by a Scottish watchmaker turned ship builder named Douglas Lapraik. Modestly called Douglas Castle—his ship business would continue the theme of his Christian name by morphing into the Douglas Steamship Company—he only used it for a few years before returning to the UK. In 1894 the castle's manager, along with about half the colony, fled Hong Kong when it was struck down with bubonic plague, and French missionaries bought it. With the fall of China to the communists foreign missionaries were no longer welcome, and so the castle was in turn sold to Hong Kong University and turned into rather splendid halls of residence.

Doubtless old Douglas made use of the third thing that Pokfulam was known for in days past, and that was its dairy herd. The only remnant of the cows that once lowed here are the bleached octagonal cow sheds that remain, nestled into a set of buildings that manage to provide the unique combination of a performing arts centre with an Anglican church. These milking parlours are more than just a bovine monument, but are instead a reminder of another one of Hong Kong's league of extraordinary Victorians, a man who managed to be the father of tropical medicine and, as an aside, a co-founder of one of Asia's leading food companies.

Patrick Manson was born the son of a Scottish laird and farmer, and reportedly a relation of the explorer David Livingston, studied medicine, moved to China, and for some reason became an expert on elephantiasis. He operated on over two hundred sufferers, including one that tried to sue him—in the style of the film Life of Brian—for destroying his livelihood as a beggar. He conducted numerous experiments on mosquitoes and anyone that could be of assistance, including his somewhat surprised gardener. As if to show he wasn't a discriminating man, he also purposefully infected his family, injecting his son with malaria to help prove that the disease was spread by mosquitoes. When he moved to Hong Kong in 1883 he busied himself not only by founding a successful private practice and setting up the Hong Kong College of Medicine, but also by establishing a herd of imported cattle to provide fresh milk to Hong Kong's inhabitants. The company he co-established, Dairy Farm, is now a major international company. As if all that wasn't enough, he also turned the course of history by securing the release from custody of Dr Sun Yat-sen, the revolutionary who would use his newly-found freedom to overthrow the Chinese Emperor and usher in a chain of events that led to the People's Republic. Not a bad list of achievements really, and that doesn't even include setting up the London School of Tropical Medicine, which he did on his return to Britain.

After an afternoon wandering around Pokfulam, it was time to head back to the Midlevels and some proper city life. Just as we were waiting for the bus, I noticed something furry and a couple of feet long lying in the gutter a few yards down the road. I couldn't work out what it was at first—it was quite mangled and bloody—but there was enough left to attempt a Google-picture identification. It looked like a civet cat, which I thought only lived in deep jungle. Well maybe they did normally, which is why this one managed to get itself run over. But it was a good reminder that Hong Kong wasn't just about people. It was still wild enough to have some life, although not all of it was welcome.

Of all the many memorable experiences of living in Hong Kong, the one I longed to forget was the cockroach crawling across my bare pink foot.

May had started with a mini heat wave and, come one evening, I stood next to the open balcony door refreshing myself in the breeze and pondering the less important things in life. Feeling something on my toes I looked down to see a blur of brown lolloping along my skin. We had already played host to a number of geckos, which we would occasionally see shooting across the wall from picture to picture and feasting on the micro-ants that appeared in the nooks and corners of the flat.

So as I noticed the creature traversing my foot I sincerely hoped it to be one of our lizard friends. It took a long, long second for my brain to shelve that idea and tell my conscience what it actually was, at which point my leg dramatically engaged and catapulted the filthy cockroach away.

Unfortunately my subconscious had not bothered to compute the direction of my kick, a fact soon realised by Aggie as the insect came barrelling towards her. Now I had always known my wife to be a woman who was quite quick in the leg department, but I had never suspected her of being capable of the awe-inspiring turn of speed which she now showed. She was up on the back of the sofa before I could even cry a warning, and able at the same time to shout the superfluous instruction "Get that thing OUT of here!" in the manner of an irate grizzly bear.

"Don't crush it! Its eggs will spread everywhere and then you'll have even more to do," was her follow-up advice as I chased after a scurrying insect with a jam jar and a piece of card. Still, at least it wasn't a rodent; neighbour Vivian told me about a woman who walked into the bedroom of her expensive Repulse Bay flat to find a large black rat perched on the cot of her newborn daughter.

Happily there is more to Hong Kong's wildlife than rats and cockroaches, although there isn't a shortage of these; there are for instance six species of rat, including one, the great bandicoot rat, which can grow to two feet in length. There are also thirty-one species of roach, plus six species of flea and seventy-eight species of mosquitoes for good measure. There are also two thousand moth, one hundred and ten dragonfly, and two hundred and thirty butterfly species that make their homes here. According to the Government, Hong Kong also boasts four hundred and ninety bird types, around one third of the total bird species in China, and an array of freshwater fish, amphibians, and reptiles. There are also eighty-two mammal types, about half of which are bats, and some of them quite exotic. Once, as we were driving over the pass at the back of Happy Valley, we spotted what looked like a jaggedly badger, but on closer inspection revealed itself to be a porcupine—but like Pokfulam's civet cat, sadly dead. There is also what was, on another memorable occasion, described to me as a "flying scorpion with green and yellow rings!

Come quick!" but which is actually a harmless three-inch lantern bug. Not only does this little insect have the most striking red trunk and beautiful white and green mottled wings, but it also has a curious meme associated with it. Despite it being a plant eater and thus not overly fond of carnivorous behaviour, locals say that if one bites you then you will die if you don't have sex within twenty-four hours. Whichever bloke came up with that particular myth would have been very popular with his friends come lantern bug season.

Despite the plethora of wildlife we didn't often see too much of it day to day as most creatures were well hidden. I wouldn't poke my head up either, not with seven million voracious humans on my doorstep; as someone once alluded, "If it has four legs and is not a chair, if it has two wings and flies but is not an airplane, and if it swims and is not a submarine, the Cantonese will eat it." I didn't meet a single local that disagreed with this, and in fact most took it as a compliment.

"We don't waste food like you do in the West," one of my colleagues succinctly put it.

Rather than spend hours out in the national parks looking for creatures, the best place to see local or foreign critters like ring-tailed lemurs, Hawaiian geese, or even a Hoffmann's two-toed sloth was at the Botanic Gardens. Hundreds of animals and birds screeched away in their fair-sized cages, under the watchful eye of an austere statue of King George VI and the park wardens that silently roved around. It was an exquisite place to spend an hour or two.

It was Saturday in early May, and although most of the blossom was gone, the trees were looking verdant and healthy. Larry and I had been thrown together for the day as Aggie had gone off to swim as part of her sarcoidosis rehabilitation, so I decided it was time to instil the naturalist in him and take him to the Botanic Gardens.

We trooped around the cages, Larry's wide eyes bulging at the sight of artificially pink flamingos and red-crowned cranes that preened and, well, craned their necks high. For some reason there were dozens of amateur photographers there, some holding cameras the size of interstellar telescopes that were, curiously given that we were in the middle of one of the most urban areas on earth, draped in camouflaged material. These men, and one appallingly coiffed woman, all sported utility waistcoats, all the better to hold the lens rubs or Teflon tripods or whatever latest gizmo they'd spent their dollars on.

Larry and I passed on, looking for some lesser spotted ice cream to munch. We found ourselves with vanilla cones in our paws looking up at the orang-utan enclosure, trying to spot the new twins that had apparently just been born. We waited for a while, crowded on all sides by eager-beaver tourists, but soon gave up when Larry sprinted off to offer his snack to an inquisitive pigeon.

We had booked dim sum for lunch and headed there via the Mid-levels wet market, dozens of food stands crammed in and around Peel Street. Chinese stall holders, young and old, male and female, and all looking rather harried with life, haggled and bargained with Filipina helpers and local housewives. Fruit, vegetables, and meat of all hues were for sale, alongside delicacies like thousand-year eggs and special funguses, giving the streets a smell that lay somewhere between a kitchen garden and abattoir. It was exciting and fresh, until, that is, we arrived at the fish stalls. There the juxtaposition with the Botanic Gardens in terms of creature welfare could not have been greater.

One of the true benefits of living here was that the local Chinese were extremely pleasant, so long as you were human. The kids didn't drop litter and attack each other with Rottweilers; the old folk were all respected and looked after; overall there was a very low level of crime. But their treatment of animals was something else entirely. Morrissey, the oddball singer, generated a fracas a while back when he called the Chinese a 'subspecies' for the way they look after animals. He may have totally overstepped the mark in the broadest sense, but anyone familiar with the operations of Mainland fur farms would not have been too damning of his comments. Vlad the Impaler and Genghis Khan would have been appalled by the photos that pop up with even the most cursory of Google searches.

Hong Kong was not in the same league at all, but there were still sights to shock. Back at the market, we stopped at a stall to peer at the fresh fish they kept flapping in water-filled polystyrene boxes. A middle-aged man, with tortoiseshell glasses, grey slacks, and a dirty white shirt said something in Cantonese to the stall holder and pointed to a succulent looking specimen. With a flip of her hand the fish was soon in a net and being passed to the assistant, a young girl with a face already ravaged by time. Remarkably, rather than dispatching the fish then and there, she picked up a thick wire brush and started to descale the poor creature as it lay suffocating in the spring air. Its flanks truly mangled but its mouth still gaping, she popped it into a cheap plastic bag and exchanged a fistful of dollars with the man. I was all for fresh food, but this was just not on.

I decided to talk to New Moon about this. I waited until a suitable gap in the lesson, when we were both bored of the book but had a little time to wait until the half-time break, to tackle her on animal welfare.

My story of the brutalised fish was met by a thin smile, then surpassed by an even more gruesome market tale of fish being filleted alive. To her this was totally traditional, as well as being a sign of a highly skilled fishmonger at work.

"You think it is better to eat dead fish?" I assumed she meant fish that had been killed on the trawler out at sea; that said, considering a well-known Chinese delicacy is to place a living lobster in the centre of a table and slowly carve thin slivers from it, I wouldn't necessarily have been surprised if she hadn't.

"Well, I don't see why the fish can't be killed humanely before you start preparing it for supper. And while we're at it, I think that some of the restaurant fish tanks are a bit dirty and crowded." This didn't go down well at all, and I had a short but forthright lecture on how it was better for diners to have fresh food than for fish to have rights. It was a question of public health, she maintained.

In good, old-fashioned English style it was all becoming a tad embarrassing, so I attempted to explain the British mentality about animals. Such as the fact that the National Society for the Prevention of Cruelty to Children was founded as an offshoot of the Royal Society for the Prevention of Cruelty to Animals some sixty years later, and still didn't have a royal title. That a story about horse meat being found in Tesco value burgers received more airtime than eighty people being slaughtered in the Middle East.

She met these anecdotes with a slight grin, but when I moved onto a description of the London memorial to animals killed in war she laughed until she almost burst. A deep, throaty laugh that welled up from the belly and caused her to blink like a peering frog.

"They had no choice? Of course they had no choice, they are animals! You are all very strange." She wiped a small tear from her eye.

Happily, at least pets were treated a little better. It might be surprising to know that, given that most people lived in flats, pets were all the rage in Hong Kong, and in particular dogs. Labradors, Golden Retrievers, local Chinese Chaus with the friendly, fox-like faces and upturned tales who have the unfortunate provenance of being originally bred for meat; apart from the occasional Yorkshire Terrier and Chihuahua, it seemed that biggest was best.

The trouble was, the bigger the dog, the bigger the dog poo. There had been a problem with this canine waste probably for as long as Hong Kong had existed, but the issue was now quite serious. Although councils helped owners out by providing 'dog latrines'—sandpits located on paths around the island which some unfortunate souls had to clean out each day—some owners still allowed their beasts to crap all over the place.

There was dog turd everywhere. I mean everywhere, smeared on all the pavements right across Hong Kong. It wasn't generally in the form of steaming piles that would arrest the passer by with their whiff and cadre of attendant flies, but instead represented by small brown pellets that lay in wait for the unsuspecting foot, or more unpleasantly, the innocent toddler to fall into. It was even worse than Paris if it could be believed, and that was saying something.

This slapdash attitude to public hygiene had, not surprisingly, raised the ire of a number of folks. Unfortunately their solution was to kill the dogs by hiding poisoned food in places the dogs would be likely to find on their walks. Seventy-two dogs had been poisoned since 1995, with two-thirds subsequently dying. Chris Patten, aka Fat Pang, the last Governor of Hong Kong, had his dog poisoned in 1997, but luckily it survived.

As the police didn't seem to take the poisonings too seriously, vigilantes were known to tour the walking routes looking for the culprits. These do-gooders—in the best possible sense if, like me, you were a fan of the old pooch—patrolled the pavements, put up warning posters, and even raised money for rewards to catch their foes. The trouble was, given the rugged nature of many of the paths and trails here, laying down poisoned meat was very easy to do and it took a lot of luck to find the perpetrators.

The easy solution would have been for there to have been a complete cultural change that made every dog walker clean up after their charges. But as the poor fish of the wet markets understood, altering animal customs out here was quite a challenge.

TWENTY-NINE

···

At the heart of Hong Kong's rowdiest area, Wanchai, is Hennessey Road. It is, quite aptly, named after one of the most chaotic governors in the colony's history. To say John Pope Hennessy, who governed between 1877 and 1883, was divisive would be a gross understatement. A thin, pale man with a prominent nose, he managed to alienate his fellow colonialists, fall out with his family and annoy his staff like no one else. His one grace was to become firm friends with the Chinese, whose lives he made strenuous efforts to improve. He would have fitted right in with the chaos and cultural intercourse of Wanchai.

Hennessey, a former Conservative MP and a trained army doctor, was actually Irish, like a great many of his fellow governors. He was sent out into the world by the Colonial Office in the wake of the Indian Mutiny of 1857, which had in part been caused by the misrule of the locals by increasingly aloof Britons. Tasked with bringing the two sides closer together, he set about his mission with gusto.

Unfortunately, much like Lord Napier forty years before, his ambition soared well above his ability, particular in the man-management department. Oblivious to his own imperfections, he came up with scheme after scheme but flitted between them so that none was seen through. His dislike of delegation led to severe micromanagement, meaning he went through his staff with quite amazing speed.

177

It wasn't only his staff that he clashed with. Other members of the Hong Kong establishment couldn't abide him. The senior General went so far as to stop a military band playing for the Queen's Birthday celebrations the Governor was holding; Hennessy had to send a begging letter to London, who obliged by forcing the General to send his music men. But it wasn't as if the Governor had any friends back in England. Colonial officials were bewildered by Hennessy's continued refusal to open their missives, let alone act on them. Official commands normally just went in the safe and stayed there, which was yet another source of conflict with his staff.

You might have thought that given his professional relationship issues he might have wanted to keep on good terms with his family. Not a bit of it. Referring to his father-in-law, a fellow colonial professional, as 'the Plague' probably didn't make them bosom buddies. His wife, Kitty, did not appear to be her husband's biggest fan either. She apparently had her own admirers, which is not a surprise given that her beauty was said to be 'out of the ordinary', according to one report of the time.

This legion of fans included the colony's most senior lawyer, who the Governor one day caught in Mrs Hennessy's boudoir, but doing nothing more than reading a museum guide, albeit containing, to his horror, pictures of naked female statues. The shock of it must have been seismic because when, shortly afterwards, Hennessy bumped into the lawyer out walking, he proceeded to beat the man senseless with an umbrella. Not what Britannia would have necessarily expected from one of her Big Chiefs, I'm sure.

Despite the hatred Hennessy generated among the Europeans, his relations with the Chinese were warm. 1870s Hong Kong was a thoroughly divided colony. One hundred and thirty thousand Chinese lived in the western slopes of Hong Kong Island while the nine thousand Europeans inhabited 'spacious houses on tree lined streets.' The enmity between the two sides was enormous, both looking down on the other with disdain.

It wasn't for nothing that the locals called the interlopers 'gweilos'—foreign devils that smelt of sour milk.

Hennessy decided to stop the unequal treatment of the more numerous contingent of Hong Kong. He attacked the night-pass system, which dictated that Chinese were only allowed out after 9pm with a lantern and a written permission slip. He then banned public flogging and branding, much to the delight of the local coolies, who started referring to the Governor as 'Number One Friend.' The Europeans, led by William Keswick, the head of the Jardines trading house, were not too impressed with this, especially as the crime rate started to rocket. The soft-on-crime approach was soon tested when eighty armed burglars sealed off a street to rob it, fending off the police and making a hasty boat-borne escape.

A public meeting was called. Victoria was now a "more unsafe town than any town of the British dominions" and something had to be done. The Europeans and Chinese clashed but soon the former had the upper hand, and so the Governor was forced to appoint a new Chinese Secretary to settle things down. Strangely enough he was a German philosopher, but Hennessy wasn't renowned for his predictable decisions.

In the end, his legacy was more than just social discord, broken umbrellas, and happier Chinese locals. It was Hennessy that planted thousands of trees to turn the original 'barren rock' into the verdant isle it is today. So although the fact that Hennessy Road had more mayhem than most was fitting, the fact that it had no trees was a missed trick.

I was now crossing Hennessey Road every morning on my way to work. The journey was always the same, involving a five minute bus ride, then a four minute tube journey, and finally a walk along an elevated walkway to my building. After a few repetitions I started noticing the same characters each time, particularly on the walkway. The bespectacled beanpole of a man vigorously handing out unknown pink leaflets, or the legless beggar dozing against the railings, obviously caught my eye. Then there was the recycling woman. With short, black, wavy hair, a round face liberally scattered with small warts, and dressed all in black, she consistently waited at the exit of the MTR station waiting to grab old copies of the free newspapers that in other cities get shoved in the bin, or more likely tossed on the floor. I wasn't normally a fan of reading the paper but her gratitude each time I gave her my tabloid was such that I took up the habit just so we could cheerily greet each other with "Jou-san!"

It was now the end of May, and I had very much enjoyed my second month of work. There was a great deal to do, but it was highly satisfying and meant that I was able to focus my mind after an extended period of idleness. I was so busy in fact that my social life had taken a decidedly lower profile, and I hadn't been out with Tom or Nick for a while. Not that Tom was partying much either—every time I spoke to him he seemed to be craving a quiet night in.

As I would have done with a new job in Britain, I spent my first day making sure that I learnt several crucial things, which were, in order of importance, the location of the kettle, the loo, and who the most important person in the office was.

To the non-office worker, the last point might seem obvious: the CEO of course! But no. Show me the company where the Chief Exec is the most powerful person in the building and I'll buy you a book on basic psychology. Steve Jobs; Richard Branson; Warren Buffet; all united by a reliance on their personal assistant. She, and it's very rare not to be a woman, will be the ultimate gatekeeper and the pathway to the leader of the business. As Charlie Sheen discovered in Wall Street, the quickest route to the boss is by buttering up the PA.

Yet in Hong Kong, the power of the PA is somewhat diluted by the existence of another breed of superwoman, namely the Office Assistant, or OA. You could dismiss their contribution by pointing out that they only order the stationery, run some small administrative errands, and pop around with a hot drink twice a day, but to do so would be a folly of the highest order. The fact that they know everyone in the office—all their comings and goings, their likes and dislikes, their relationships with other colleagues—gives them an almost superhuman power to influence. This was augmented by their control of the kettle. As an erstwhile colleague once said, "She who wields the coffee holds the throne."

Since arriving in Hong Kong I had heard numerous tales of careers blunted and even derailed by not playing the OA game. One poor sap, a fresh-off-the-plane partner at a well-known management consultancy, made the fateful error of taking against the Office Assistant for not bringing him the right biscuit or some such triviality. It was the end of him. Not in the blaze of glory that perhaps drunkenly pissing on the Chairman's desk might achieve, but in a more subtle way: death by a thousand slow, almost imperceptible cuts. This particular chap first knew something was wrong when the work started drying up. He had found himself at the bottom of the pile when new clients came knocking, their enquiries always sent to his fellow partners by the receptionist, who naturally took the OA's side. As such his team, bored by the lack of work, started to leave. His invitations to the office social events never seemed to arrive. His tea always tasted rubbish. And soon it was him alone. He was back in Canada by the year-end, broken and looking for a new job.

I did not have long to wait to meet our OA on my first day, for ten minutes after I had sat down at my desk, idly chatting with my new colleagues, a glass trolley appeared at the doorway pushed by a small, middle-aged woman with short hair and a kind-hearted smile. She had come to inspect her latest recruit. Within a minute she knew exactly who I was, thanks to the simple question of what kind of hot drink I liked. It was said that OA's categorised their boys and girls by their choice of beverage, and so I had to make the right decision. Unfortunately as I was new I didn't yet know the rules so just had to go on taste, which for me was good, old-fashioned English tea.

"OK, good choice for you." I had obviously passed muster.

OAs aside, there was not too much difference between a Hong Kong office and a London office. For a start, they were all housed in the steel, glass, and marble buildings that had taken root around the world like a particularly virulent form of Japanese knotweed. Inside, receptionists waited with hands over buzzers ready to admit DHL couriers, general visitors, and, of course, new hires. Workers sat on open-plan floors, sub-divided by fabric-covered partitions upon which were pinned photos of loved ones, old to-do lists, and the ubiquitous office phone number sheet. Conversation was kept to a murmur, except for people fetching a glass of water or that one person in the corner who insisted on cracking jokes first heard in 1987.

The one critical difference in Hong Kong was the lavatory, in that they were all kept locked. There were many rumours as to why this was the case, but the two most popular ones were that it was to stop women being attacked, or to prevent "old people stealing the toilet paper to sell on the streets" as a Chinese friend once told me. Whatever the origin, it was a practice that drove many of my expat friends crazy. As one twenty-something noted, the morning after a couple of bottles of wine and a dodgy kebab, the last thing you needed was to rush to the loo only to discover that you had left your key on your desk.

THIRTY

....

Every so often, especially when beer is involved, you will find yourself party to a conversation that is notable only for its absolute dullness, such as the question of if roundabouts were really invented in Britain, the merits of one-handed data entry, or perhaps whether the lift-close buttons do actually work.

The lift question was one that I had not sought to answer, but unfortunately had taken up a good chunk of a student evening that I was never going to get back. Little did I know that some fifteen years later I would be able to clarify with certainty that the buttons weren't just part of elevator decoration, but served a serious purpose in giving Hong Kongers an extra second or two of extra productivity each day. Everyone was at it, closing doors in the faces of young and old alike, just to make sure that they didn't have to wait any more than they really had to. It was a fervour bordering on the fanatical for some people. Heading back from lunch one day I noticed a young woman heading into the lift about ten yards ahead. As she entered she spun around to face the doors, making eye contact with me as she did. In most other countries this social interaction would have been followed by her waiting all of three seconds for me to enter the lift, perhaps even smiling at me to show that she didn't mind the micro-delay. Not here. A look of solid determination appeared beneath her glasses, and I knew the game was on. I started to sprint the last few yards as her finger frantically jabbed at the button.

The doors started to close, so I lunged forward, only just managing to shove my shoe into the gap and stop her. The doors sprung open again as I looked her in the eye, smiled, and pressed the door open button to allow some others to join us. Petty, yes, but highly satisfying too.

Wearing a sandpaper shirt would have been less irritating than this obsession with closing the doors. But to the locals this was completely normal, and none of my colleagues seemed to mind having the door shut on them. What really freaked them out was sneezing. In those post SARS days a sniffle, a cough, a wheeze, or a throat clear all had the ability to make the locals tremble. Western nations may have a dread of terrorism, but here the fear narrative was being stuck in a lift with a bird-flu victim. People had been known to faint on particularly long elevator rides as they tried to hold their breath for the duration.

Lift annoyance aside, one particularly pleasant part of my job was my colleagues. Although one could hardly have described the office atmosphere as anarchic, or even febrile, there was a buzz about the cubicles. A source of this was perhaps the way that most people went out to lunch each day with each other, in groups of two, three, or more; bonds were therefore socially refreshed each day.

As most of the staff were Chinese, the usual lunchtime haunts were the mom-and-pop local restaurants that existed by the hundred on the back streets of Hong Kong, no matter how smart the neighbourhood. These came to life early in the day to serve the huge breakfast rush; for some reason the locals seemed allergic to eating anything at home first thing, opting instead for a bun of some kind, a plate of noodles, or bowls of steaming congee ladled out for a few dollars a go.

My team seemed to have fallen in love with two particular establishments, one nicknamed the 'Red Restaurant', the other the 'Yellow Restaurant.' This was down to the decor rather than any reflection on the use of food colouring. The average cost of a huge plate of rice and meat at one of these places was about $40 (£3.20), which felt like a good deal. In fact it was possibly too good a deal. Most cheap food came from China, where there were plenty of stories about contamination. Heavy metals were of particular concern, especially mercury which had killed a few locals recently. There was also the habit of substituting food products for artificial, chemical alternatives, like fake eggs, but also more worryingly milk powder. One well-known scandal back in 2008 had involved powder being adulterated with melamine, a chemical better known for use as a fire retardant or the basis for laminate flooring. Three hundred thousand babies were poisoned, and fifty-four thousand hospitalised, with six dying from kidney complications. The reason behind the adulteration was apparently to make the powder seem to have a higher protein content. Watering down milk powder was nothing new though. A few years before, diluted milk powder had caused the death of thirteen babies from malnutrition.

If Mainlanders were capable of messing with the safety of infant milk powder then there was every likelihood of unscrupulous food manufacturers doing the same with a wider variety of products. As one of my Chinese colleagues put it, "I'll believe in the Chinese Dream that our President has mapped out for us when I can believe in the quality of my food." Who knew what was really in our lunches.

Health fears aside, the lunch experience was good fun, albeit slightly different to that in the UK. Neighbour Vivian explained the difference between a Chinese and a Western restaurant.

"In the US or UK they make their money from the drinks; in China the owner makes money from the food. So they have to get everyone in and out as quickly as possible." She was sure that this was why poisoning from cooked food was so rare, because with such a high turnover of customers no ingredients ever sat around decaying.

This desire to get as many punters through the door as quickly as possible was a novelty to me when I first visited London's Chinatown, and a well-known restaurant called Wong Kei, or Wonkees as everyone knew it. It was the first time in my life that I had been made to sit next to strangers in a restaurant, and the experience was apparently also quite novel for the other six people crammed onto our table. What a neat marketing idea I thought. Until I came to Hong Kong, which is when I realised that cheek by jowl was the way that everyone ate here. In Wonkees everyone tried to do the English thing and be polite by attempting small talk with the neighbour, but not in Hong Kong. The etiquette here seemed to be to totally ignore the unfamiliar folk opposite and carry on with the meal as if seated at your own table. This was a bit more difficult when sat in proximity to untidy eaters, especially when pieces of food flew from their lips into my bowl. This happened to me a few times, and there was no choice but to ignore it.

We never had our own table at the Red Restaurant. This was a family owned place, and it felt like it too. The walls may have been untouched by decoration, the room neon-bright, and the fish in the tanks decidedly on the deader end of life, but it was jolly and vibrant and fun. The owner, and father of the family, strode around in a tatty green t-shirt, faded blue trousers, and black rubber boots that made him resemble a homeless docker. He sounded bad too, his voice resonating like a badly oiled chainsaw. Working alongside him were the rest of his family: the daughter that cleaned the cutlery in a large red bucket; the wife that ran the cash register; the brother, replete in a ninja black headband, that chopped up the sizzling slabs of pork; and the cousin who took the orders, and who was unmistakable for both the red-checked lumberjack shirt she wore every day, as well as the truly atrocious memory that necessitated endless trips back and forth from the kitchen to confirm exactly what the customer wanted. The tables were round, Formica, and cheap, with a box of Kleenex in the middle rather than napkins. Sitting alongside the random other customers we munched through the dishes that were plonked in front of us—and which sometimes, if we were lucky, coincided with what we had ordered—listening to the family argue and squabble amongst themselves. It had the ambiance of a home, and to be honest it probably was, no matter what the building regulations dictated.

The food may not have been the best, but it was an enjoyable place to spend half an hour. That said, many of the better quality culinary experiences, in terms of food and setting, were to be found at the outer extremes of Hong Kong, away from the main working areas. This is where Aggie and I headed now.

THIRTY-ONE

....

One Saturday in early June we decided to head west. The summer heat was starting to reach uncomfortable levels, so we set off early before we could be caught in the open and roasted alive by the midday sun. We were heading to an old outpost of Hong Kong called Tai O, the western-most settlement of Lantau Island, which meant a convoluted journey by taxi, ferry, then bus. A Chinese friend had said it was "the Venice of Hong Kong, but not as pretty, nor as Italian, and it is a bit run-down" and with a description as enticing as that it had to be seen, no matter what the distance.

What the casual visitor probably didn't know was that Tai O was where Anglo-American military cooperation took root. Having been really not too fond of each other since the small matter of the Revolution, not to mention the War of 1812 when the White House was burnt (and, I might add, when Washington's defenders developed heatstroke thanks to their rapid retreat from the advancing British Redcoats) it took an unnoteworthy sea-borne incident to bring the sides back together; something the Japanese, Germans, North Koreans, Serbs, Iranians, Iraqis, Libyans, and many others have no doubt been ruing ever since.

In 1855 Pacific Ocean corsairs were flourishing, with Chinese Long John Silver wannabes pockmarking the various coastlines with their hideouts. Many a piratical junk, perhaps the descendants of Stanley's Pirate Cheung, sallied forth to seize unsuspecting cargo ships, whether local or Western. It was hard to believe that it would have been such a problem given the current tranquillity of the area, but letters and anecdotes from the mid-nineteenth century show that being taken captive was a relatively common hazard of sailing the nearby seas. Conditions in captivity weren't overly comfortable, as shown by the experience of Fanny Loviot, a Frenchwoman taken by pirates near Macao in 1854. She was kept for a week in a narrow dark hole below decks, accompanied by a menagerie of spiders, woodlice, and rats, until eventually being rescued by British sailors.

Having marauders snatching young ladies from their boats was obviously not something that was going to be tolerated for long. One gang made the unfortunate mistake of nabbing a couple of merchant boats being escorted by the Royal Navy, spurring a ferocious response. Quite why this event spurred the British to reach out to their American naval cousins is unclear, but they did, and soon sailors from the USS Powhatan, HMS Eaglet, and HMS Rattler were combining forces to destroy the pirate menace. They did so rather effectively too, killing over five hundred brigands for the loss of only nine dead and several wounded. This simple act created history as the two navies came together for their first joint operation. What is more remarkable is that the US commander, William J McCluney, actually fought against the British in 1812.

With a nod to the town's nautical past the first thing we did when we arrived in Tai O was take to the sea, but in search of mysterious sea mammals rather than bandits. We stepped onto a fast, pencil-shaped motor boat that was skippered by a sea-ravaged man with enough wrinkles to cover an elephant, and with a surge we were out on the waves looking for pink dolphins. These marine mammals were well-known inhabitants of the neighbouring coastline; well, apparently, because we saw none that day, and not a single person we knew had ever spotted one. But the ride—zinging over the waves at a high rate of knots, bumping and bashing along—was worth the $20 fee alone.

From the water it was apparent to see that Tai O's best days were behind it. What used to be a centre of smuggling, salt production, and fishing looked to have been reduced to a down and out tourist haven, its famous stilt houses looking in strong need of a lick of paint and some extreme structural renovation. It was a significant reminder that not everyone in Hong Kong was able to shop at Chanel.

The town may not have been in the best upkeep, but the atmosphere was pleasant indeed as we stepped through the market-stall-lined streets. The shopkeepers, many of whom specialised in selling dehydrated fish and turtle parts—desiccated swim bladders were in particular evidence, alongside whole dried sharks and rays—gave a cheery "Jou-san" as we ambled through the narrow lanes. There was even one old lady, craggy but smiley underneath a wide-brimmed bamboo hat, who was handing out free cups of a special type of tea. We accepted the small porcelain cups without really knowing what the dark, sweet liquid was, but thought it very refreshing indeed.

At one point we came across a series of wide, flat wicker baskets that were covered in what looked like a pinky-purply paste, reminiscent of dyed wallpaper glue, baking in the heat. As we approached we soon understood what it was by the smell, an odour so strong that it sat in my nostrils for an hour afterwards. Tai O was famed for its shrimp paste, a reputation built, I could only assume, on its taste rather than its smell, because it stank really, really bad.

We soon had an opportunity to taste the paste by heading for lunch at the Tai O heritage hotel, one of the main reasons for visiting the town given its culinary reputation. Situated in the old police station, its bleached colonial arches and stiff white flagpole made it stood out prominently above the water. Unfortunately the service was also noticeable, but for all the wrong reasons. We waited around twenty minutes to be served despite there being only four other guests, and a further half an hour waiting for our drinks. In that time one of the waitresses managed to kick Larry's high chair on three separate occasions, once so hard that he was nearly upended, and without once apologising. We were both glowering with rage when the plates came, so our moods were hardly lightened to discover that the only aspect of the hotel worse than the staff was the food. I had ignored my nose and gone for the shrimp paste rice, but it turned out that I should have relied a little more on my olfactory sense. The rice tasted like stale, salty vomit, and despite being ravenous, I just couldn't force it down. We left the hotel pretty disappointed on all fronts.

Notwithstanding our Tai O culinary experience, June had started off with a little leap of happiness, kicking its heels and whistling a tune. Everything was going well, and had been for a few months now. Larry was enjoying school, and had started swimming and football lessons which he thoroughly relished. Aggie had started to feel better, and no longer coughed so hard that she feared vomiting up her own lungs. As for me, well it was summer, I had a great job, was playing tennis weekly now the hockey season had ended, and there were plenty of parties to go to. All in all, we were at last feeling settled and happy to be in Hong Kong for some time to come.

Then most of our friends left.

We headed back from Tai O to have dinner with Nick and Laura at the Globe, a pseudo-British pub in Soho that, apart from being shaped like a long box with attached lavatories, actually sold good food and beer. Sitting at a booth and enjoying an above-par steak pie, Nick somewhat changed the mood by telling us that his father was terminally ill.

"So obviously we'll be moving back home soon."

This was all terrible. We felt very sad for Nick of course, and we would be sorry to see them go, but these things happened here. Back in the UK friends were normally for life, or at least a good length of time. But Hong Kong was, as everyone knew, a place of transience. Friendships could often be like a flare: bright, but short-lived. What we hadn't expected was that so many of our new friends would be leaving at the same time, and that the social life we had spent nearly a year fomenting was about to evaporate in a matter of days.

A day or two after Nick and Laura's announcement I had lunch with Tom at a delightful restaurant in Wanchai called The Pawn. It was set, as the name implies, in an old pawn shop, and was perhaps the only piece of private colonial architecture left in the area, a stone-colonnaded pearl in an architectural desert of glass and steel. I hadn't seen Tom for a while, so was looking forward to catching up on his latest exploits. What I wasn't expecting to discuss was his departure. Life had seemingly become too decadent, even for him

"I think if I stay here it will kill me," he confessed. My natural nightlife instincts had been heartily curtailed by my family life, but Tom knew no such boundaries. Comparing the youthful and vigorous face that he arrived with just one year before with the exhausted, semi-haggard visage that appeared before me now I could see his point. He had been thoroughly Hong Konged.

Given that he was blown out by partying so hard, Tom departed Hong Kong without much of a do, and very soon after our Pawn lunch. I had one last drink with him—and it was a solitary pint—whilst we reminisced about the fun we had endured, and then he was off. As was the way with passing pals, there was every likelihood we would never see each other again.

With Nick and Laura, the goodbye was different. Rather than quietly disappear into the ether, they were determined to leave with a bang. They decided on going to the races, which was always going to be fun.

When the British first arrived in Hong Kong they soon noted that there was not too much flat land, apart from, that is, a small valley at the north of the island that was home to a rice paddy or two. The Army, always looking for a good spot to parade its soldiers, set up camp there, but soon the men were falling like flies—or even mosquitos—as malaria swept through their ranks. Officials soon turned the area over to the dead, and a number of graveyards were established there, hence the adoption of the euphemistic 'Happy Valley' name.

Someone once said that when the French arrived in a new country the first thing they did was to build a bakery. For the British it seemed that their Asian expansion was marked by the number of racecourses constructed. Normally the settlers waited a few years to get things going; in Australia the oldest recorded race was twenty-one years after the First Fleet arrived, and the Singapore Turf Club wasn't founded for twenty-three years after Raffles had kicked things off. In Hong Kong, by contrast, racing progressed at a characteristic gallop, with the track being laid down at Happy Valley a mere five years after the colony was founded. It said a great deal for the enthusiasm for racing of those early settlers that they were prepared to risk malaria for a night watching the horses.

The racecourse revealed the same cultural differences between Chinese and Westerner that we had seen in Macao's casinos. When we entered the track, paying all of $10 (80p), we would have thought that we were in a European-only enclosure, as hundreds if not thousands of white faces jostled around us drinking beer, barely glancing at the track just in front. But when we looked behind us we saw tens of thousands of Chinese folk sitting still, staring intensely at the course and with only a couple of cans of coke between them. These were men and women who had come to bet, and only to bet.

As the elders of Macao had shown, gambling was the lifeblood of many a Chinese man or woman. Apart from betting on football, the Hong Kong Jockey Club was the only other form of betting allowed, and so it funnelled a huge amount of desire and luck; it was said that each horse race had over US$100 million riding on it. In fact, the Jockey Club took so much money that it was both the largest taxpayer in the SAR—over ten percent of all Government revenue, in fact—and, as a non-profit organisation, the largest provider of charity funds, averaging over HK$1 billion a year. This was an excessively successful outfit.

Nick and Laura held court trackside as all their friends chatted and reminisced, sipping beer and soaking up the noise of bets lost and won. The horses galloped past, their multi-coloured jockeys flashing through the gaps in the rail and being cheered on by the crowd. Occasionally one of us would hop off inside to place a bet, normally something astronomical like $50, or on a rare occasion even go to collect some paltry winnings. At a pause in the race schedule a rock band started playing somewhere near us, and was soon surrounded by swaying race-goers, all of a Western nature. The local Chinese meanwhile sat unmoved up high, plotting their betting strategy for the next race. It was really a tale of two worlds.

If there's one thing though that binds cultures together it is the love of winning. Such is the addiction to gambling here that a whole raft of betting tools have been invented for the track. There are seven types of bet for single races alone—win, place, quinella, quinella place, tierce, trio, first four, and a quartet—the details of which were too much for limited gamblers like myself. There were also All Up and Cross Pool All Up betting, which I didn't even try to understand. This was betting on a super scale.

It was a quinella that gave Nick and Laura the perfect send off. As the results were announced on the electronic scoreboard Nick let out a roar and lifted his wife into the air, a touch of worry across her face until she realised the reason for his yelling. In years of coming to the races, this was the largest win they had had, and so they drew a close to their stay in a rather suitable way. The champagne flowed for the rest of the night.

THIRTY-TWO

....

O n Friday 2 June 1995 a hairdresser named Herman went swimming near Clearwater Bay. He headed into deep water and no doubt splashed around a while, at which point a six-foot-long shark decided to drag him underwater, and remove the flesh around his left thigh for good measure. Not surprisingly he died, although he was prescient enough to give a little shout before he went down so the sunbathers on the beach knew where to fish out his body.

This might have been thought of as a touch of bad luck. After all, millions of swimmers, surfers, divers, and snorkelers use the sea each day and only a handful are chomped. But Herman should have known better, because only the day before, and in the same location, a scuba enthusiast had his leg bitten off by a shark and also died. Most people, when ordered to stay out of the water because a man-eating shark was on the prowl, would probably have decided to skip their swim and head for a jog instead. Not Herman though.

What made these deaths extraordinary was that this was not the first cluster of shark-related deaths at the same spot. Two years before, in fact to the very day, a forty-two-year-old man was taken a short stroke away from where Herman met his fate; twelve days later a sixty-one-year-old man met the same fate. And in 1991, again in June, three locals were devoured within a few miles of Clearwater Bay. All in all, a total of ten people were eaten in this four year period, including a fisherman who had his arm bitten off, and the most unfortunate of all, a woman who was playing beach volleyball and went into the water to retrieve her ball where she was nabbed. The person that spiked the ball into the sea wouldn't have slept easy after that.

To add to the conundrum, shark attacks in Hong Kong had been extremely rare up to this point. In fact, the first recorded mention of one was in 1945 and involved a police sergeant named either Jackson or Goldie, depending on which report you read, who tragically had just been released from four years of living hell in a Japanese internment camp. Some people have all the luck.

Even more heartrending were the shark fatalities of the 1970s, when numerous refugees from the Cultural Revolution attempted to swim to Hong Kong and were picked off on the way.

Many of our Chinese friends and colleagues here in Hong Kong were directly touched by the Cultural Revolution. This was communism at its very worse, when Chairman Mao decided to purify the Chinese Communist Party by forcing millions of evil bourgeois and intellectuals into manual labour and had tens of thousands put to death. Education and healthcare basically stopped, as doctors, nurses, teachers, and pupils were sent out into the countryside for re-education. The unrest didn't stop until the death of Mao in 1976, followed shortly after by the arrest of the Gang of Four, the nominal leaders of the terror, including Mao's wife, all of whom were sentenced to life in gaol.

We lost count of the number of people who told us about how they, their parents, or their grandparents had managed to escape the terror and flee to the British Colony. One notable story was recounted to us at a South African-style braai hosted by Cameron and Chlöe at their home in the eastern and very Chinese district of Shau Kei Wan, which despite its down-at-heel look was an energetic neighbourhood complete with Michelin-starred curry house. Cameron's colleague Philip was a lively fellow, with short, neat hair and skin that looked highly moisturised, who sported metrosexual designer clothes that made him look quite different to the rest of the assembled crowd. We had a light-hearted chat about his travelling shenanigans and the various girlfriends he apparently had across Asia, before stumbling onto his family history. Philip's mood became reflective as he told us how his grandfather had been broken by Mao's henchmen, the Red Guards, for being a teacher.

"He was sent into the fields but never came back. He died from the stress." His grandmother saw the writing on the wall and decided to flee with her young daughter to Hong Kong.

Even if the Revolution didn't kill you it still had an impact immeasurable in Western terms. Wang, a man we met at church, quietly told us of the horror that his family had been through during this time. His father had disappeared, leaving only he and his mother living in a couple of rooms in the southern city of Guangdong. For reasons that he didn't explain, and about which I didn't enquire, his mother's mental health disintegrated at the height of Mao's turmoil.

"Each day we only had a few small bowls of rice to eat, and maybe some vegetables. We had meat just a few times a year, and absolutely no dairy. I was really concerned about my mother, and I convinced myself that she needed some milk to make her better. I had heard that there was a man who owned a cow in the countryside outside my city, so one day I borrowed a bicycle and went to look for him. After nearly a day I found him, but there were five other people there also wanting milk. Luckily he had enough to give me a glass, so I gave him my money and took it home to give to my mother." Wang was fourteen at the time.

Eventually he managed to escape China by teaching himself English and geology while working in a butcher's shop; one day he smuggled himself into an international academic conference and met a British professor, who thankfully arranged for Wang to study in the UK.

"If I hadn't been to that conference my life would be very different now," he remarked, with very little in the way of bitterness. He didn't say what happened to his mother.

For those without the luck and academic drive of Wang, such as Philip's relatives, there were several ways that people could make the journey out of China. Surely the most perilous must have been to swim to the most easterly island of Hong Kong, called Ping Chau, which lay just a short paddle from a peninsula of China proper. Unfortunately for those fleeing, the water between the peninsula and the island was deep and clear, and so was home to a good number of large, aggressive sharks. Quite a few of the refugees—"dozens, if not hundreds" according to neighbour Vivian—were eaten. It just goes to show the true nature of the vile depravity of the Cultural Revolution that they were willing to risk a grisly end rather than stay in China.

Back to 1995, and something clearly had to be done to stop the sharks. The government sprang into action, obviously having seen Jaws and realising that the Amity Island head-in-sand approach was not going to work, not with the headlines now hitting the world's newspapers. Shark nets were installed at all thirty-two officially kept beaches, and renowned Australian shark hunter Vic Hislop was brought in to see if he could find the culprit. That all he apparently did was to drink Victoria Bitter in the Kangaroo bar for two weeks didn't seem to bother his employers, probably because they hoped the killer would already be long gone.

Unfortunately this was not the case. On 13 June a woman named Wong was eaten, just eleven days after Herman. A witness report from the time noted that 'the woman was screaming for help and waving her right hand in the air. Then the screams died down and her body began to float on the water and the sea turned red. We saw the shark bite her.'

A legacy of these deaths was that the government had become pretty twitchy about shark sightings. Every time a large fish was spotted the sea was evacuated and, for some reason, the beaches shut. This did seem somewhat excessive because, to my knowledge, no one had ever been attacked by a shark whilst on dry land, but that was the way they wanted it.

It was with this background lodged somewhere deep in my mind that we went to Stanley beach one sizzling Saturday in late June. The sand was its normal crowded self, with thousands of people crammed onto an expanse of sand the size of a tennis court. In one corner was a taped-off area which was even more densely populated, with several hundred Indonesian domestic helpers who had been herded there by the Chinese authorities so that they couldn't mix with the general public. They didn't seem too perturbed by the experience and were the jolliest folk on the beach, singing songs and taking photos of each other in their colourful hijabs. Yet for them, not being allowed into the sea had its upside that day.

The heat felt like a hammer to the head, so I was nominated by Aggie to take Larry into the water to cool him down. Avoiding the many other parent-child combinations splashing in the shallows, as well as the flotilla of plastic cups, takeaway containers, bags, and random pellets that littered the breaking waves, I carried him into the deep on my shoulders. Every so often there would be a strong tug on my earlobe forcing me to turn one way or the other, which of course he found hilarious. Soon my ears felt distinctly elongated.

After a while the aural pain and the constant barrage of rubbish against my body got to me and, ignoring Larry's pleas, I took us out of the water. No sooner had I reached terra firma then there was a loud announcement over the tannoy. It was in Cantonese so I didn't understand a word, and just continued our slow march up the beach. Suddenly dozens of locals started streaming past me, leaping out of the water like fleas from a dead dog. Soon the only bodies left in the sea were a couple of Chinese and a bunch of Europeans, who were bobbing around like softly frying whitebait.

Call me Sherlock, but I instinctively knew what it was; I placed my hand straight up on my head, Jaws-style, to warn Aggie. Sure enough, all was revealed a couple of minutes later when the tannoy voice switched to reedy American English.

"A large fish has been spotted. Please leave the water immediately."
Three minutes after that a third announcement was made, only this time
in Mandarin. If ever there was a symbol of Hong Kong's antipathy to
Mainlanders then this was it.

Given my longstanding issues with sharks—started by an aunt who
thought an eight-year-old boy would be perfectly happy watching towns-
folk being eaten alive—I would have heard those words with the panic
of a man waking up from a deep sleep to find the crematorium burners
being started around him. But given my untimely prescience I instead
serenely oversaw the rescue operation, all the while singing to myself
"Show me the way to go home."

What was really great about the whole evacuation thing was that all
the swimmers, who were the first to be notified of the feeding machine's
presence, were behind a shark-net. Others not so fortunate to be behind
the protective shield were left entirely to their own devices, and for what
seemed like hours. This included, four or five hundred yards offshore, a
kayak school for kids merrily plying their way through the choppy waves,
overturning and waiting an age for their chubby teacher to come and
rescue them. Then there were the elderly windsurfers flopping about at
the other side of the bay, and the lone paddle boarder making his oblivious way across the waves. It was a Hollywood pastiche of potential victims. Eventually a lifeguard made his way over to them, but it took
forever to clear them all from the sea.

Although the fish in question ended up being a harmless whale shark,
I resolved to stay out of the water for a long time to come.

THIRTY-THREE

....

Hong Kong's sharks weren't restricted to the marine variety. When we were living at Central 88 I noticed one morning that dozens of protestors had formed an orderly line alongside the road. Dressed in a mixture of lounge suits and tracksuits, the mixed bag of old and young were chanting loudly in Cantonese in answer to a woman yelling something through a microphone. A large banner strung up on the railings next to them revealed the focus of their anger—and believe me, they sounded pretty damn pissed off, with spittle flying and arms waving—to be Citibank. Or 'Citicrook' as one of the signs indicated, a slogan adorned by the picture of a red sickle with bloody globules dripping from it. I asked a fellow voyeur what it was all about, and was told that the bank, in the true style of a ruthless financial predator, had somehow ripped them off though mis-selling, but neither he nor I really understood the issue. At least the slogans—another one read, in a fine piece of wit, 'Shittybank'—were memorable.

As the Occupy movement of 2012 and 2014 proved, protests in Hong Kong were not unknown. In fact, they have been spreading over the last decade or so. According to the police, in the year 2002 there were around two thousand protests; nine years later that figure had risen to over seven thousand. The locals raised their arms up about everything, not just about the larger questions like democracy. Demos against everything from errant financiers to anti-incineration plants have been seen, often populated by professional protestors who make a lot of noise but rarely damage anything. We also noticed a vicious battle between supporters and detractors of a Chinese group called 'Falun Gong', which played itself out in huge poster campaigns at strategic locations like overpasses and the Star Ferry terminal in Kowloon. Graphic posters of supposed victims of Chinese state torture lay juxtaposed with youth council warnings of the 'Evil Cult Falun Gong'. The pictures may have been stomach-churning, but they were representative of an effervescent debate.

That there was so much local protest would have come as a surprise to the many doom-mongers ahead of the UK's 1997 transfer of Hong Kong, back to a communist Mainland not overly known for its toleration of dissent. As might be imagined, a loss of free speech was just one of the many things that quite simply petrified the locals, of whatever ethnic background, in the run up to handover.

In theory Hong Kong should have remained British 'in perpetuity', as per the terms of the Treaty of Nanking in 1842 and the subsequent Convention of Peking eighteen years later. In fact, it was only Hong Kong Island and Kowloon that were permanently under Britannia's cloak. The New Territories had only been leased for a ninety-nine year period that was due to expire in 1997. Although in theory the UK could have insisted on keeping hold of the island and the opposite peninsular, the fact that so much of the territory's infrastructure, especially water, was located in the New Territories meant that it was in practice quite unfeasible for Hong Kong to have continued shorn from its hinterland. It was with this understanding that Margaret Thatcher entered into negotiations for the handover of Hong Kong back to the Motherland, culminating in the 1984 Sino-British Joint Declaration.

On the surface, history might be surprised that there was any nervousness ahead of handover. Even though the British position was weak because of the New Territories lease position, the Sino-British Joint Declaration was favourable to Hong Kong, its unique status being preserved for a guaranteed fifty years under the 'one country, two systems' pledge offered by Beijing. In addition, China itself was not the same communist monster that had caused the Cultural Revolution and the even more deadly Great Leap Forward only a generation before. It had been blessed by the strong and reforming leadership of Deng Xiaoping, a man so hard that he had survived not one, but two purges by Chairman Mao and seen his son paralysed by extremist Red Guards when he was thrown out of a window. Deng's decision to effectively end communism and replace it with 'capitalism with Chinese characteristics', had ushered in three decades of liberal-ish economics that had transformed the country. Whereas once China had a total GDP the size of Spain and a per capita GDP marginally above Haiti, it now has an overall economy second in size only to the US. Five hundred million Chinese have been taken out of poverty along the way. This was not the China that most Hong Kongers had fled.

Yet in the 1990s, Hong Kong was scared stiff. Many individuals and companies took the opportunity to escape, with over a million people reported to have emigrated to countries like the UK, Canada, Australia, and even, so it is said, Ecuador and Gambia. Jardines, that stalwart taipan, moved its headquarters to Bermuda, and HSBC—probably Hong Kong's most powerful institution—transferred itself to London. It is fair to say there was a great deal of angst, and the site of the green-uniformed People's Liberation Army storming into Hong Kong at the handover ceremony did little to soothe the nerves.

Yet as the current crop of protestors showed, the post-handover reality that we found was quite different to that prophesied. For a start the Mainland influence here was limited to backdoor deals and the odd outburst by Hong Kong pro-Beijing politicians. Many of these didn't do themselves any favours by being so slavishly loyal to the Motherland that they lost all local respect. One classic, ridiculous example was Ma Lik, a former teacher and active proponent of communism, who, when asked his views on the 1989 Tiananmen Square slaughter, told astonished journalists that because some people managed to leave the square it was not, in actual fact, a massacre. It was reported that he then went on to ask the Education Department to redefine the word 'massacre' as being where over four thousand people had died, conveniently making sure that the Tiananmen Square protests—where, not coincidentally, an estimated four thousand people died—failed to make the grade. Stalin would have been proud of his revisionism.

Politics aside, there were a few other Mainland influences that had crept in. The school system for one had been sinofied, and Mandarin was now used for announcements on the MTR, alongside the traditional Cantonese and English voices. But on the whole people still felt very distinct from the Motherland. Polls consistently showed that the majority of locals considered themselves to be Hong Kong citizens rather than Chinese citizens.

Mainland influence also hadn't suppressed the local democracy that had been established late in the day by Governor Patten. Come election time—for example for the District Council—we saw the candidates launch campaigns based around superficially innocent single issues, with new bus routes being a particular staple. That didn't mean the races were without bite. In the 2012 Chief Executive elections—which, it must be noted, were voted for by a one thousand, two hundred strong election committee rather than the people themselves—the leading contender, Henry Tang, was cut adrift by his supporters, including Beijing, when it was revealed that he had built an illegal basement in his house. He then proceeded to courageously blame this construction on his wife, the same wife who he had told the world he was cheating on a little earlier in the campaign. Who said chivalry was dead?

Whilst Mainland influence had not been overbearing, British influence had not waned in the way that it might have either. According to a lecture I went to with the British Consul, UK investment in Hong Kong is now many times higher than it was pre-1997. None of the place names have been changed, and the statues of King George and Queen Victoria still stand resplendent. Even the electrical plugs are the same. Sure, the post boxes may now be plain green rather than the British red of old, and the Jockey Club and police may no longer have 'Royal' in their names, but around a hundred British policemen remain in police service, and buildings still find themselves named after, or at least by, the Royal Family. York house in Central, built several years after handover, was opened by the Duke of York, Prince Andrew.

It is not surprising that British influence remains strong when, according to the British Consulate, there are over two hundred and fifty thousand British citizens living in the SAR, plus a further three million British Overseas Nationals. Quite how long Beijing would tolerate this many 'foreigners' on its soil was the subject of several debates I witnessed, but for now non-Chinese influence was fully entrenched in the territory. If not only for the sake of food contamination and street navigation, this was a good thing.

THIRTY-FOUR

....

J uly started with an urgent phone call from my mother.

"Sam, can you talk?"

"Sure, but what time is it there? It must be one in the morning—is everything OK?"

It turned out it wasn't. My sister had been embroiled in a violent incident, generating a predictable family panic. It all took its toll, on both her and my mother, who was naturally very stressed.

Staying up for many a night to deal with this family issue was a stark reminder that Hong Kong was not exactly next door to our wider family. We knew that living six thousand miles away from them would not be easy, but given that we Skyped the grandparents most weekends we had kind of grown used to the separation. This jolt though had reminded us that it is simply not so easy to return to the UK quickly in the event of something going wrong with the family. Nick and Laura had seen that with his father's illness, and they had decided it was best to move back home rather than deal with it from afar.

The family was a critical distinction between East and West. In China kin was everything. Witto once introduced me to a Chinese financier at a lunch who, to be frank, had more money than he knew what to do with. He could have afforded to have done absolutely anything that he wanted to, whenever he chose. Yet all his spare time was spent with his extensive family, admittedly in a luxury tower block that he owned. Almost every festival was celebrated with a family feast, and it started young; parents held a 'hundred-day birthday party' for new born babies, and it was relative party-time ever after.

This focus on close family is ironic given that, despite the West's economy having recently faltered, there are still so many Chinese living abroad: fifty million by some counts, a figure five to ten times higher than expat Brits. Yet although they may have moved to foreign shores, many a Hong Kong Chinese expat will still return periodically, especially if there is a family celebration of some kind.

With Western, particularly Anglo-Saxon, families there may not be the same never-yielding kinship bond, but it didn't mean that we weren't fond of those we had left behind. With a few of Aggie's elderly relatives also ailing, health concerns were mounting on both sides of the family, and so naturally we started to wonder if it would be better to move back to the UK. On top of this was the lingering concern about Aggie's health, and so not surprisingly the suggestion of leaving Hong Kong after only a year was one that we discussed at length. True, we had both settled into our jobs, and Larry was enjoying nursery, but did this trump family and health?

These discussions coincided with a summer holiday back to the UK. As we packed up our suitcases we knew that we would have to use our two weeks back in England to decide what to do with our future. As The Clash once said, London was calling, and it was time to weigh up whether to stay or go.

We agreed that, although family and health were of course really rather important, we would use the time to compare the other aspects of life that we valued both in Asia and in Europe. One of these was the sheer safety of Hong Kong. My sister's altercation had reminded us of how secure we were in our Eastern enclave, compared to a great many places back home, even the London Underground. The police in Hong Kong were excellent. True there was an awful lot of counterfeiting, but that didn't tend to put you in hospital or mug you for your mobile phone. On the whole the streets were generally safe, at least for the ex-pat. There were no gangs of feral youths roaming the underpasses for a start; teenagers were generally at home studying hard or playing with their Wii consoles. Of course there was some crime, but the statistics revealed just how different its prevalence is to London, a comparably sized city. In 2011 for instance there were seventy five thousand, nine hundred and thirty-six reported crimes of all types, with seventeen murders and ninety-one rapes. Greater London, in roughly the same period, registered more than eight hundred thousand, which included one hundred and twenty-four homicides and three thousand, two hundred and seventy-nine rapes. And London wasn't even the most dangerous city in Europe.

Around half of all Hong Kong's crimes were thefts, which reflected well on the type of crime most expats were exposed to. There were the occasional pickpocket incidents—a British guy was rumoured to have clobbered an aspiring wallet-stealer on a crowded tram some years ago—but it was burglary that was of most concern.

Back in England most people would assume that leaving a top floor window ajar would not be a major problem. Given the rise in obesity it would be a miracle if a would-be burglar had the puff to put a ladder up against the wall, let alone shimmy up a drainpipe. Not so in Hong Kong. Many of the locals were pretty lithe, which if you were a housebreaker was a good shape to be. Even lofty flats with locked windows were vulnerable to the skinny burglar, as our friends the Mitres found out.

It was the start of July, and we had joined a group of families for an early morning picnic on South Bay beach, a stretch of gloriously empty sand at the bottom of the island that had become a favourite with us. Like many of the 'official' government beaches there was a café, and a lifeguard, and a shower block, and the regulation shark nets. It was also home to a unique demographic mix, at least in terms of Hong Kong beaches, being a place that attracted not only families but the resident gay community too.

It was difficult to believe that it was only in 1991 that homosexuality was decriminalised in Hong Kong. Whilst you couldn't find anywhere like San Francisco or Manchester's Canal Street area here, it was not uncommon to see men holding hands with each other in certain places like Soho, or indeed South Beach. We had arrived at the beach before anyone else, but as one of the fathers barbequed the bacon ready for our breakfast the crowds started turning up en masse. A magazine review had described how the families normally took up one side of the South Beach, and the gay crowd the other, but they obviously hadn't been here recently because very soon the parents and children were totally intermingled with young male couples of every ethnic mix sunning themselves. One interesting figure was a solitary German with tight blonde hair and even closer cropped swimming trunks, who spent hours marching up and down the sand checking out the talent in a manner that even Liberace would have found gauche.

After a swim to and from the floating platform anchored in the middle of the bay, we settled down to munch our bacon butties and watch the kids try to force-feed sand to each other. It was then that we heard the unfortunate news from one of the families there, Andy and Jodie Mitre, a Yorkshire/Devon mix with a cute girl the same age as Larry. They had had the misfortune to be the only people in Hong Kong that we knew of who had been burgled. Despite being on the third floor of a block of flats, in a pretty nice part of the island, some thieves had shimmied up the drainpipe and yanked open the windows with screwdrivers. Andy, luckily without the family, had returned to the familiar scene: clothes tossed around, electronics missing, jewellery evaporated.

"But the third floor's pretty high. You can't have been expecting that," I helpfully pointed out.

"That's nothing," replied Andy, almost gleeful, "on Wednesday the guys came back and broke into someone's flat, and this time on the tenth floor."

At least they weren't home when it happened. One Swiss couple we heard about had just arrived in Hong Kong and were eating dinner when an armed Indonesian gang burst into the flat. They tied up the husband and threatened the wife and baby, before making off with money and valuables. Then, a few days later, they came back—but this time the wife and baby were in the flat alone. History doesn't relay what happened next.

Luckily for us, these stories were very much the exception. Yet in the early years, Hong Kong had a far rougher reputation. One of the first governors, a fearsome Irishman named Sir Arthur Kennedy, was a keen advocate of stern punishments. He had arrived in the colony in 1872 and, like many of his time, was a tough old bastard. He had served in the British Army, followed this with a short stint administering relief to the victims of the Irish potato famine, and then headed off to be the governor of Western Australia. The locals of Perth and the surrounds didn't take too kindly to old Kennedy, complaining that he was too draconian.

The fact that some of the hardiest settlers in modern day European history were complaining about the strictness of their governor says it all. These were a group of colonists trying to make a new life in a new town nine thousand miles from home, surrounded by desert, sea, and numerous fauna that would think nothing of turning them into a tasty snack, and their governor was too tough even for them. Hong Kong wouldn't have known what had hit it.

When he arrived in this corner of China he encountered a colony where crime was all the rage, especially burglary. All he wanted to do, according to one report, was to make the colony into a 'place where an Englishman could dwell in peace and security.' The administration was smoothly run, so he could turn his attention to what was apparently his main interest: law and order.

If, during the nineteenth century, you were keen on learning a bit about being authoritarian then there were not many better places to study than in China. John Keay's excellent China: A History is packed full of the worst punishments for the most minor of crimes, from Imperial times up to near the present day. Most Brits these days would consider transportation to Australia for stealing a piece of bread an over-the-top punishment, but how about executing your entire family for an inopportune word at court?

One favourite punishment of the old emperors was to execute all the relatives of a criminal, to nine degrees of kinship. These included:

- The children of the offender
- The grandchildren of the offender
- The offender's living parents
- The offender's living grandparents
- Siblings and siblings-in-law
- Uncles of the offender, as well as their spouses
- And last but not least, the offender himself.

This was an extreme punishment in any context, but many of the execution orders were for the slightest insult, anything in fact that could have been interpreted as 'treason' against the Emperor.

Happily for women, there were certain periods of China's history when females caught up in this familial slaughter could choose slavery instead of death. An easy choice, one might think. Certainly a quick beheading would be thought preferable by many to a life of brutal, enforced servitude. Yet this was the kicker, in that it wasn't a clean and simple death for many. Instead, the preferred method was 'death by a thousand cuts.' This is not, as one might imagine, a thousand serrations of the body. An inch long cut here, a two incher there. No, it was far, far worse than that. It was instead the slow removal of parts of the body over an extended period of time.

Chinese law did not stipulate exactly how the process should be carried out. So fortunately for executioners wanting to experiment with their task—there's surely nothing more boring than being stuck in a dull, repetitive job—there was considerable variance shown. Some would have it easy:

"The executioner, standing before him, with a sharp sword makes two quick incisions above the eyebrows, and draws down the portion of skin over each eye, then he makes two more quick incisions across the breast, and in the next moment he pierces the heart, and death is instantaneous. Then he cuts the body in pieces", wrote an Australian, G. E. Morrison, in 1895.

Others wouldn't have liked it so much. The unluckiest would have had their eyes poked out so they couldn't see what was coming, increasing the psychological terror. They would then have had all the little appendages cut off, one by one, including toes, fingers, thumbs, ears, nose, tongue, and genitals. Oh, and breasts too if you were a woman that had erroneously chosen not to go down the slavery route. The executioner would then move onto the chunkier pieces of the body, like shoulders, thighs, and the like. Finally, he would start to cut off whole limbs, followed some time later by a coup de grâce to the heart.

One somewhat foolhardy man, a scholar by the name of Fang Xiaoru, was notable for having been taken to a whole new level of punishment. He managed to arouse such wrath in one particular emperor that he became the only man in Chinese history to have ten degrees of his family exterminated. The scholar himself got off lightly with a mere severing at the waist, which was rather unfair considering that he had upped the ante by daring this particularly bloodthirsty tyrant to "go ahead with ten" rather than the customary nine degrees. In addition to his blood relations and their spouses, the executioners worked their way through all of his students and peers as the tenth group; a bad day at school in anyone's book. Altogether, eight hundred and seventy-three people were said to have been executed.

Modern day China is considerably more civilised. For a start, no one has been killed by a thousand cuts since 1905. Yet China still executes more people than the rest of the world. Amnesty reported that one thousand, seven hundred and eighteen people were put to death in China in 2009, which although gratuitous, was actually down from an estimated ten thousand in 2005. These high numbers come about partly because of the wide range of crimes that could lead to capital punishment, some of which are unique to China. Before the recent revision of the criminal code, tax fraud and other economic crimes would have seen you taken to the execution van. And yes, this was literally a van where people were executed by lethal injection. Firing squads on the other hand were reserved for 'normal' crimes like murder. China in all had fifty-five crimes punishable by death, although this no longer included those found guilty of killing pandas, no doubt much to the chagrin of the WWF.

For those Chinese people who liked a good gawp at those about to die, a new TV show had started. For all its gross, indecent existence, at least Judge Judy didn't end with the defendants being lined up against a wall and actually shot. But this was exactly what they had in China. The host, an attractive woman drolly nicknamed 'Beauty with the Beasts', interviewed murderers just before they were executed. There was certainly the appetite for it, with the programme being watched by forty million people.

Getting back to Hong Kong, Sir Arthur Kennedy took many of these Chinese traditions as inspiration for his law and order crackdown, but in a very watered down way. He increased flogging before the crowds on Queen's Road, and introduced the branding of criminals behind the ear. Troublemakers were expelled from the colony. One of his last acts as Governor was to increase jail sentences and to decrease the quality and quantity of food served in prison, so as to "make the life of prisoners in Gaol, and of Chinese prisoners especially, as distasteful as it can possibly be made." His rule was well received; Sir Arthur was the only governor given the honour of a statue erected by public subscription.

THIRTY-FIVE

....

G iven our interest in crime and punishment, we decided to follow our bacon breakfast at South Beach with a visit to the Police Museum. Sitting in an isolated part of the Peak, the first thing we noticed was the brand new ramp that allowed the wheelchair-bound to enter the premises. Except that to get to the ramp they would have to be bumped up a dozen or so stairs; such is the way of much of Asia. Even at Aggie's work, which is a company with a fully developed social conscience, the wheelchair access is terrible, with the route actually including an escalator.

Once we had passed the disabled person filter we paid our $20 entrance fee to the bespectacled man behind the counter, who, like so many civil servants, had attended the Soviet school of customer relations. There was no speaking, no acknowledgement of our presence other than a hand rising up to take our money and another passing our tickets. He just stared. I felt like poking him in the eyes to see if he was hypnotised, but thought better of it and watched Larry sprint off instead.

The museum actually had a great deal to see, just to rub it in to those stranded in their wheelchairs outside. A large collection of disarmed weapons, old motorbikes, and forged banknotes covered the walls. A notable exhibit was a Standard Chartered note which said 'Ten Dollars' in letters but had '$500' in numbers on the bottom corner, designed for ripping off Mainland Chinese who couldn't read Latin script; cultural understanding at its criminal best.

Yet the standout exhibit was undoubtedly the tiger head hung proudly high on the wall, its features in a perpetually surprised snarl. Just below it was a pre-stuffing photo of it in all its glory, albeit freshly shot and quite dead. The beast was dispatched back in 1915, curiously enough just after a series of articles in the local media discussing whether or not there were any tigers living nearby. The authorities didn't believe the Chinese villagers at first, and sent up a couple of policemen to see what all the fuss was about. I imagine the constables were pretty grateful to know that they'd answered idle press speculation in the affirmative by proving that the tiger did actually exist, right before it ate them. As with most animal attacks, humans had the last laugh by blasting it to kingdom come, then mounting it in a museum. Still, at least it wasn't eaten, which was the sad fate of the last Indochinese tiger in China. The poor animal was killed in a southern Chinese nature reserve in 2009 by a villager, who took the feline carcass back to his family for dinner.

My tiger mulling was interrupted by a sharp tap from one of the museum employees, who angrily pointed to Larry happily running his toy car over some of the exhibits. He wasn't damaging them, but was causing enough anxiety to make our security friend annoyed. Our visit was cut short when he pointed us to the exit.

In comparison to civil servants, especially museum-based ones, we found the police to be very approachable. In fact their kindly attitude, at least to gweilos, made them feel a little like the old British bobby. I'd been mildly rebuked for many a thing by police in Russia, Argentina, Bolivia, Serbia, Montenegro, Cyprus, Norway, even (well, especially) America, but never once had I felt intimidated by the coppers here; quite the opposite in fact. One late night return from work saw my taxi driver drive in circles around the Midlevels in a crude but effective effort to drive up the fare price. To add insult to injury he then refused to hand over my change. I had only been ripped off by forty or so dollars but

Sister Yi, who happened to be working nights that week, called the police. Two young and bespectacled officers arrived within minutes and asked us both what the issue was. After a brief, frank, but calm discussion the taxi driver agreed to hand over the change and excess fee to me, before one of the officers, with cropped hair and a wan expression, ordered me to bed. My last view was of the driver being closely escorted to the police van, no doubt for a bit of an informative chat.

Another thing going for the police here was that they were clean. Whereas in China the constabulary were said to be the type of people that paid for their Chinese New Year presents with the bribes they received—"It's always dangerous driving just before lunar holiday, you can get pulled over for anything," said New Moon—here in Hong Kong they were more respected. Yet this had not always been the case.

I had been invited to lunch by Witto again, and found myself sitting between a number of old Hong Kong hands, all of them 'lifers' that had no intention of heading back to the UK or from wherever they originally hailed. On my right was Bob, a guffawing Englishman with wild, sandy-grey hair and jowls that sank down to his collar. It was he who told me the story of the biggest crook in Hong Kong Police history, a man who ironically shared a name with one of the main characters of the prison comedy Porridge.

Chief Superintendent Peter Godber was one of the colony's most famous policemen, decorated for bravery in a nasty and generally unknown part of Hong Kong's history, the 1966–67 riots. These euphemistically titled 'disturbances' were actually pro-communist bomb attacks, riots, and general violence throughout the colony that left over fifty dead, including, horrifically, an eight-year-old girl who was killed by a homemade bomb made to look like a gift. Godber had been a steadfast figure throughout this period and was lionised by many for his performance and commitment to duty. Until one day the anti-corruption branch discovered four point three million dollars in his bank account.

Luckily for him, Godber had been well trained. Knowing the game was up, he arranged for his wife to leave on the next plane, then quickly followed, using a special police permit to bypass immigration where the police were waiting for him. His escape didn't go down well with the local population who were annoyed, to say the least, that the most senior policeman charged with graft had been able to avoid arrest.

Godber was, unfortunately, only one of many policemen involved in the take. There had been decades of the police accepting money from crooks, who knew that so long as the general public was unharmed the fuzz would look the other way. A former policeman that I met at the Football Club told me that when he arrived at his desk on his first day he opened his draw to find a wedge of cash lying there. Naturally he told me that he didn't take it, but many others did, which is why the anti-graft agency, the Independent Commission Against Corruption, had had such a field day arresting numerous Godber clones, both Chinese and British. One of their most prized scalps was Godber himself, who was eventually forced to come back to face justice and join his TV namesake inside.

THIRTY-SIX

....

B ritish expats, even those on the run, can be critical creatures.
Newspaper letters pages, especially those of The Telegraph
and The Daily Mail, are bloated by complaints about the country—the dogs, going to, etc.—but none are more venomous than those
written in Sydney, Limoges, or even Hong Kong. It was time for our
summer holiday, and to be honest we were quite looking forward to seeing whether our time out East had made us into one of these letter-
writers, or on the flip side created such an amount of longing that we
would decide to come home after just a year. It was going to be an important few weeks.

At the heart of our discussions about the future was the list of reasons for which we had moved abroad in the first place. Cheap childcare,
good jobs, safety, and a sackful of adventures were all ours, it was true,
but at what cost? Health and family were two parts of life that didn't take
kindly to sacrifice, and yet this was exactly what we were doing. We
needed some time away to make up our minds as to where our futures
lay.

Our first impressions of the UK, admittedly through the depressingly
humdrum lens of Heathrow arrivals, was that everything seemed so rickety and grey compared to our new home. The sky, the atmosphere, the
suits; it was all just drab, and the architecture exceedingly twentieth-
century.

When we had lived in London the Heathrow Express had seemed like the height of rail travel, but even this looked, well, if not second rate, then in second place behind Asia's efforts. And the Tube—wow, the less said the better. If Cecil Rhodes had been able to compare the undergrounds of Hong Kong and London he perhaps wouldn't have declared that "to be born English is to win first prize in the lottery of life." The driverless trains of our new home were never late and their sleek insides resembled the alimentary canal of a robot—clean, functional, aluminium. In comparison, London's tube felt like a rundown 1970s sitting room, with gaudy coloured fabric and a nasal voice apologising for delays that seemed to spring straight from Abigail's Party.

Above ground the situation was different. For a start the air quality was significantly better, and blowing my nose didn't leave my handkerchief looking like I'd spent the last six months working in a coal mine. The architecture too was way different, in both style and in attitude. The city's low-rise buildings resembled the bankers and barristers that inhabited them: short, broad, and very expensive. We may have preferred the energy of Hong Kong's Blade Runner cityscape, but the power of London—although not quite what it was—shone across every marble window-sill. Asia felt rather nouveau in comparison.

There were some differences that only a Hong Kong expat would notice, like how wide the pavements were. Oh, the bliss of having space to amble without bumping into someone every two seconds. Hong Kong must have had some of the narrowest sidewalks in the civilised world, which was a thorough impediment to walking with purpose and speed. The supercharged climate—thick and hot and wet—didn't ease perambulation either.

The climate was another significant difference between our two potential homes. Dr Johnson once said that "when two Englishmen meet their first talk is of the weather." From a foreign point of view this is an extraordinary thing. Why, when Britain has some of the most boring meteorology on the planet, would its inhabitants speak of it so regularly? It's the equivalent of two Belgians tipping their hats and launching into a discussion on their famous brethren. But what a relief this mediocrity was; there was no anxiety about typhoons or black rain, and you could walk to work without arriving looking like you'd spent a day fully clothed in a Turkish bath.

It wasn't just London's infrastructure that felt antiquated; the rail journey to Dorset was almost enough to set us both weeping. The train was an absolute shocker, being smelly, tatty, and so full that there was no room for our suitcases. Our bags, perched in the corridor, were continually kicked by people on their way to the overpriced and understocked buffet car. At least the staff were pleasant, which made a nice change from many parts of the world, but this wasn't particularly satisfying compensation for our luggage being used as footballs. It was reflective of a general issue with the UK, that the infrastructure was old and tired. Why though would this matter? Aggie and I discussed this as we rolled through the countryside, and realised that it reflected a difference in attitude. The new rolling stock of Hong Kong was an indication of a diverse outlook, one focused on an ambitious future rather than stuck with a 'make do and mend' approach that blighted so much of Blighty. It was quite normal to read in the British newspapers missives from America-based expats commenting on the can-do approach that they loved so much in their adopted homes, but we had seen that this was the case in Asia too. There was something indescribably refreshing to be sat amidst a continent forging ahead, where drive and determination took centre stage, where moaning that "it can't be done" was kept to the periphery. Although there was a healthy and increasing amount of talk in the UK about a positive future, it was still way behind the Asian experience that we were enjoying.

Despite the grumbling on attitude and trains, we spent a happy few weeks seeing our friends and family, based in the countryside, and rejoicing in dry-feel skin and cleaner lungs. It was extraordinarily refreshing to be amongst the long-standing familiar and, jet lag aside, we came to the end of our stay rested and happy. There was however still a major elephant in the room: would we be staying in Hong Kong?

We hadn't really discussed it other than our first train journey, and it took a question from my father-in-law to flush it out into the open.

We were sitting under a falling sun, the garden shadows stretching over our plates, which were overflowing with home cooking. The beans, potatoes, and tomatoes from the garden all had a virginal taste that we had missed for a year. The sausages were from Lincolnshire, the beer was from Dorset, the company from a long and missed circle of the closest family and friends one could hope for. At this incredible moment of happiness, he put down his glass and asked us quite simply, "Where is your home now?"

By the time it was dark, and the meal was over, we knew the answer. All of this was a mirage, a false vision of England that we were in danger of falling for. The UK was wonderful when you don't have to commute, live there during winter, or have children under five, but for now every indicator of well-being told us that Hong Kong was the place for our family to be. We'd just have to make sure our lungs didn't give up on us in the meantime.

ABOUT THE AUTHOR

Sam Olsen was born in the UK but has spent much of the time living and working in different countries: eight to be precise. He has written numerous articles on travel and current affairs. These days Sam lives in Hong Kong with his wife and two boys.

Visit
www.samolsenasia.com
to find out more about Sam and Hong Kong.

ACKNOWLEDGEMENTS

I am deeply indebted to the many people who have contributed to this book. This is a very long list, as can be seen from the cast of characters within, but in addition to this disparate group I must also thank: Ted Thomas, Stuart Wolfendale, Mike Smith, Neville Sarony, Will Gibson, Tessie Gascon, and my aunt Claire Lister. All mistakes and misquotes are my own.

I should also mention my parents, who inspired me in my global outlook in the first place – thank you.

And of course my fantastically supportive wife, without whom none of this would have happened; and my boys, who keep me entertained at even the most stressful of times.

AUTHOR'S NOTE

Hong Kong is a small place. In the event that some people might not want their foibles and actions revealed through my clumsy hand, a few names have been altered and one or two events merged. But the spirit remains true.

MAP OF HONG KONG

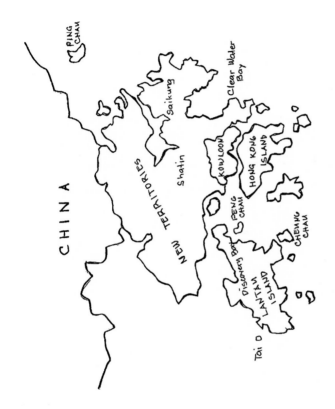

MAP OF HONG KONG ISLAND

CPSIA information can be obtained at www.ICGtesting.com
Printed in the USA
BVOW03s1042190516

448743BV00005B/167/P